AF324671

H. G. Wells's
The Time Machine

H. G. Wells at the time of publication of *The Time Machine,* 1895.

H. G. Wells's
The Time Machine

A Reference Guide

John R. Hammond

Westport, Connecticut
London

Library of Congress Cataloging-in-Publication Data

Hammond, J. R. (John R.), 1933–
H. G. Wells's The time machine : a reference guide / John R. Hammond.
p. cm.
Includes bibliographical references (p.) and index.
ISBN 0–313–33007–7 (alk. paper)
1. Wells, H. G. (Herbert George), 1866–1946. Time Machine. 2. Literature and science—Great Britain—History—20th century. 3. Science fiction, English—History and criticism. 4. Time travel in literature. I. Title.
PR5774.T53H42 2004
823'.912—dc22 2004050966

British Library Cataloguing in Publication Data is available.

Copyright © 2004 by John R. Hammond

All rights reserved. No portion of this book may be reproduced, by any process or technique, without the express written consent of the publisher.

Library of Congress Catalog Card Number: 2004050966
ISBN: 0–313–33007–7

First published in 2004

Praeger Publishers, 88 Post Road West, Westport, CT 06881
An imprint of Greenwood Publishing Group, Inc.
www.praeger.com

Printed in the United States of America

The paper used in this book complies with the Permanent Paper Standard issued by the National Information Standards Organization (Z39.48–1984).

10 9 8 7 6 5 4 3 2 1

Copyright Acknowledgments

The author and publisher gratefully acknowledge permission for use of the following material:

Excerpts from *The Time Machine* are reproduced by permission of A. P. Watt Ltd. on behalf of the Literary Executors of the Estate of H. G. Wells.

From *H. G. Wells,* by John Batchelor, Cambridge University Press, 1985. Reprinted with the permission of Cambridge University Press.

From "The Publication of *The Time Machine* 1894–5," by Bernard Bergonzi, *Review of English Studies,* February 1960. Reprinted with the permission of Oxford University Press.

From *The Hero with a Thousand Faces,* by Joseph Campbell, Paladin, 1988. Reprinted by permission of HarperCollins Publishers Ltd. Copyright © Joseph Campbell, 1988.

From *A Dictionary of Symbols,* by J. E. Cirlot, Routledge & Kegan Paul, 1981. Reprinted by permission of Thomson Publishing Services.

From *H. G. Wells,* by Michael Draper, Macmillan, 1987. Reprinted by permission of Palgrave Macmillan.

From *A Dictionary of Modern Critical Terms,* by Roger Fowler, Routledge & Kegan Paul, 1987. Reprinted by permission of Thomson Publishing Services.

From *The Definitive Time Machine,* by Harry M. Geduld, Indiana University Press, 1987. Reprinted by permission of the author.

From "The Significance of Weena," by J. R. Hammond, *The Wellsian,* no. 18, Winter 1995. Reprinted by permission of the Editor of *The Wellsian.*

From *The Logic of Fantasy: H. G. Wells and Science Fiction,* by John Huntington, Columbia University Press, 1982. Reprinted by permission of Columbia University Press.

From *Editor: A Volume of Autobiography,* by Kingsley Martin, Hutchinson, 1968. Reproduced by permission of PFD on behalf of the Estate of Kingsley Martin. Copyright © Kingsley Martin, 1968.

From "The Logic of 'Prophecy' in *The Time Machine,*" by Robert M. Philmus, included in *H. G. Wells: A Collection of Critical Essays,* edited by Bernard Bergonzi, Prentice Hall, 1976. Reprinted by permission of the author.

From *H. G. Wells's Perennial Time Machine,* edited by George Slusser, Patrick Parrinder, and Daniele Chatelain, University of Georgia Press, 2001. Reprinted by permission of The University of Georgia Press.

Every reasonable effort has been made to trace the owners of copyrighted materials in this book, but in some instances this has proven impossible. The author and publisher will be glad to receive information leading to more complete acknowledgments in subsequent printings of the book and in the meantime extend their apologies for any omissions.

Contents

Preface

The first novel of a writer who subsequently achieves literary renown is always of intrinsic interest, since invariably the author in his earliest work expresses much of his personality and attitude to life. In Wells's case an examination of *The Time Machine* is peculiarly rewarding, for the writing of it represents not simply his literary apprenticeship—the process through which he transformed himself from a little-known journalist to an imaginative writer—but his first attempt to embody in fictional form his deeply felt convictions concerning the nature of man. It is of fundamental interest to the student of his work and has always been the most discussed and most celebrated of all his scientific romances. Of all his vast output of fiction it is *The Time Machine* that seems certain to ensure for Wells a permanent niche in literary history.

Its importance goes far beyond its stature as a work of fiction. Wells's scientific romance is now acknowledged as a key text in the history of ideas, for the concept of time travel has exercised a profound influence on human thought. Moreover, the novel has made a seminal contribution to the ongoing debate concerning the future course of evolution. As a work of futurology, a literary text, an imaginative romance, and an allegory on the human condition it has exercised a potent influence on generations of readers.

The Time Machine is widely studied in universities, yet there is comparatively little critical material available of practical use to students. The student wishing to engage with this text needs a reference guide to assist him or her in getting to grips with the novel. What is needed is a basic guide that offers an overview of the novel, places it in its literary and biographical context, examines its use of language and imagery, and summarizes its critical reception during the century and more since its publication. This *Reference Guide* aims to fill this need.

It begins with an introductory chapter that traces Wells's life up to the publication of *The Time Machine*. Of particular relevance is the account of his early life, his reading and literary ambitions, and the impact of T. H. Huxley and Uppark on his imagination. Chapter 2 explores the content of the novel with a chapter-by-chapter plot summary. Chapter 3, "Texts," examines the novel's genesis and traces the evolution of the novel from its earliest version published in 1888 to the publication of the text we know today in 1895, noting the significance of *The Time Machine* as Wells's first novel and the care with which it is composed.

Chapter 4, "Contexts," examines the background to the writing of the novel, including the literary and cultural context, the impact of science and invention, the hierarchical nature of Victorian society, and the bearing of Darwin's theory of evolution on its conception. This chapter also discusses the novel's significance as a work written at the end of the century, when fiction was increasingly preoccupied with speculation concerning the future.

The next chapter, "Ideas," takes a close look at the novel's major themes, including the idea of change, utopia and anti-utopia, the extinction of man, and a history of the future. It also looks at the significance of *The Time Machine* from the point of view of Wells's psychology, noting its relevance as a study in disentanglement. This chapter also poses the question "what happens next?" and looks at the reasons why Wells never attempted to write a sequel.

Chapter 6, "Narrative Art," analyzes his literary craftsmanship, closely examining the imagery, language, and narrative techniques employed in the novel including Wells's use of irony, classical and romantic imagery, and the symbolism of dreams. This chapter also looks at the significance of Weena, a character who plays a pivotal role in the novel, and at the central importance of the white sphinx.

Chapter 7, "Reception," focuses on the publication of the novel, looking in particular at the circumstances surrounding its launch, its critical reception, and the significance of the early reviews that appraised the story from literary, scientific, prophetic, and moral standpoints.

The *Reference Guide* concludes with a glossary and bibliographical essay. The essay surveys critical and scholarly approaches to *The Time Machine* during the twentieth century, noting Wells's own attitudes to the novel and to the idea of time travel, the beginnings of serious academic scrutiny of the text, and the main lines of discussion emerging since Wells's death in 1946. The bibliographical essay also looks at critical editions of the novel and its importance as one of the founding texts of science fiction.

I hope that this *Reference Guide* will be found useful both by the student and by the general reader. I have tried throughout to bear in mind David Daiches's observation that literary criticism "is not an end in itself, but a means to greater understanding and appreciation of literary works." If this guide encourages more readers to return to *The Time Machine* and to follow it with heightened insight and enjoyment, my end will have been served.

A NOTE ABOUT EDITIONS

Page references to the text of *The Time Machine* in the following chapters are to the World's Classics edition of the novel, edited by Patrick Parrinder (New York: Oxford University Press, 1996). Quotations from *The Time Machine* are cited parenthetically within the text.

1

Introduction

I once told H. G. Wells and, after reflection, he agreed with my analysis, that at least two people struggled inside him, Herbert and George. Bert reacted; George dreamed.
—Kingsley Martin, *Editor: A Volume of Autobiography* (1968)

In the spring of 1888 an unknown young man named Herbert George Wells submitted the fragment of a novel to the journal of his former college in London. It was published in three installments under the title *The Chronic Argonauts*. It is a strange, gothic tale describing an eccentric inventor who claims to travel through time on a machine called the *Chronic Argo*. The author realized the imperfections of the story and over the next few years continued to revise and reshape it in the hope that one day it would find a commercial publisher.

Let us take a closer look at this unknown author.

BEGINNINGS

He was then a thin, fair-haired young man who was already aware of deep divisions within his own temperament—divisions that were to fracture his work throughout his life.

He had been born at Bromley, Kent, in 1866, the son of Joseph and Sarah Wells, who kept a crockery and hardware shop on the Bromley High Street. Joseph was a vigorous, untidy, outdoor man who had formerly been a professional gardener; he was unconventional and skeptical. In contrast his wife Sarah was deeply religious and orthodox; she believed the greatest virtues in life were respectability and devotion to duty. She was determined that her three sons—Frank, Frederick, and Herbert George—should all become drapers, as she regarded this as a most gentlemanly occupation.

Both in his public and private life H.G. was to be pulled in opposite directions by these competing drives—toward duty and responsibility on one hand and toward waywardness and skepticism on the other. This is evident in much of his writing and was to surface, for example, in *Love and Mr. Lewisham* and *The History of Mr Polly,* both of which feature a hero who is torn between conflicting drives. It is even more evident in his short story "The Door in the Wall" (1906), where a successful politician is torn between the pursuit of his career and a quest for an enchanted garden.

The young H.G. was a precocious boy, much given to reading, drawing, and writing. At home there were books including the works of Washington Irving, Dickens and Chaucer, George Eliot's *Middlemarch,* bound volumes of *Punch,* and an edition of Captain Cook's *Travels*. He wrote later: "The home was poverty-struck and shabby but not unhappy; if food was sometimes rather short there was plenty to read, for Joseph Wells had a taste for reading and would go to sales to pick up a cheap lot of books whenever opportunity offered."[1]

As a boy he wrote and illustrated a number of narratives told in comic-strip form, one of which, *The Desert Daisy*, ran to ninety pages and was published in facsimile in 1957.[2] *The Desert Daisy* is notable for its irreverent attitude to institutions and conventions. Wells pokes gentle fun at the government, the monarchy, the army, and the church, and he shows a deep interest in the details of warfare. It also reveals a fascination with the mechanics of publishing, including as it does a "Preface to the First Edition," an "Editor's Preface," "press notices," a "Preface to the Second Edition," and a "Summary of Contents." It is a remarkable achievement for a boy of thirteen and reveals that already he had a keen interest in writing.

In 1880 the Wells household fell apart. Joseph was now heavily lame as a result of an accident (he had fallen from a ladder while pruning a grapevine). Hitherto he had been able to supplement the meager shop income by acting as a cricket coach, but the injury to his leg meant that his cricketing days were over. In the meantime Sarah, who had formerly been a lady's maid at Uppark, West Sussex, was offered the post of housekeeper at the great house. As she had always disliked the life at Bromley she had no hesitation in accepting the post, leaving Joseph to cope on his own in the shop and thrusting her youngest son H.G. into the world of employment.

Wells left school at fourteen and after a series of "false starts" in life, including working in a chemist's shop and a brief trial spell at a drapery shop in Windsor, his mother insisted that he should be apprenticed as a shop assistant at a drapery store in Southsea, near Portsmouth. Wells endured the long hours and tedium for two years but then rebelled, insisting that he be allowed to cancel his indentures and resume his full-time education.

He walked the seventeen miles from Southsea to Uppark in order to plead his case with his mother. He was desperately unhappy, for it seemed to him that he was trapped in a dead-end occupation (shop assistants at that time had to work a thirteen-hour day) with little prospect of advancement. Clearly he felt he had reached a turning point in his life and that he must convince his mother of his determination to improve his lot.

With great reluctance Sarah Wells agreed, though inwardly she must have felt that he was making a grave mistake, and in September 1883 at the age of seventeen he joined the staff of Midhurst Grammar School as an assistant master. He did so well there that he won a scholarship to the Normal School of Science (now the Imperial College of Science, Technology, and Medicine) in London, where he commenced full-time studies in September 1884.

He was fascinated by the teeming possibilities of science, and as a student at Midhurst Grammar School and a biology student under T. H. Huxley, he worked extremely hard to master a wealth of scientific knowledge. He was consumed with a vision of life as an evolutionary process in which "every day and every hour, every living thing is being weighed in the balance and found sufficient or wanting,"[3] and inspired by a sense of all that science might do for human well-being. At the same time he was distracted by romantic drives, in which he was beckoned by visions of beautiful goddesses, the poetry of Shelley and Keats, and the prophetic writings of William Blake. The scientist in him led to ambitions of being a teacher or a research student, of finding a practical outlet for his fascination with biology. The romantic in him led him to write poetry and fiction, to dream of lovely encounters and find enchantment in the works of Whitman and Rousseau. This divergence between rational and emotional, classical and romantic, is evident in all his work.

Wells's student years at South Kensington were characterized by much speculation regarding the nature of the fourth dimension. On 14 January 1887 he heard a paper on "The Fourth Dimension" given by his fellow student E. A. Hamilton-Gordon to the Debating Society (later printed in the *Science Schools Journal*). It was this paper that gave Wells the germ of the idea of a four-dimensional geometry:

> We must first of all imagine a figure in a plane to be endowed with senses of sight, touch, and hearing. Now let a solid body approach the plane; so long as it remains outside the plane it will be absolutely invisible, but as soon as it enters it, there will become visible that section of the solid that is made by the plane; and if the solid continued moving, different sections would be continually presented to view; finally, when the solid had passed through the plane, it would suddenly and mysteriously vanish, and the thought-endowed plane figure would be unable to conceive whence it came or whither it went.
>
> Moreover, if there were some impenetrable object in the plane, such as an impassable line, so that figures in the plane could not pass it, it would form no obstacle whatever to a solid body, which would pass through, or rather, round it, quite unconsciously; so that it could enter enclosed places that would be quite unattainable to bodies moving in the plane alone.[4]

What Wells does in *The Chronic Argonauts* and later in *The Time Machine* is to seize on this idea, let his imagination play upon it, and cast it into a literary form through the device of time traveling.

Although Hamilton-Gordon himself rejected the notion that time is the fourth dimension, he had undoubtedly planted a seed in Wells's mind. By speculating on the nature of the fourth dimension and raising the possibility of constructing a geometry based upon it, he provided Wells with the initial spark that eventually became *The Time Machine*.

The fundamental notion Wells derived from discussions in the Debating Society is that "the normal present is a three-dimensional section of a four-dimensional universe" and that the only difference between the time dimension and the others "lay in the movement of consciousness along it."[5] This was the seed that germinated in his mind and that bore such spectacular results in his first novel.

As early as 1885, when he was nineteen, he had presented a paper to the student Debating Society under the title "The Past and Future of the Human Race," showing that his thoughts were already turning to the future of humanity. This was eventually published in a thoroughly revised form as "The Man of the Year Million," in which he boldly speculates on the probable course of evolution:

> The theory of evolution is now universally accepted by zoologists and botanists, and it is applied unreservedly to man. Some question, indeed, whether it fits his soul, but all agree it accounts for

> his body. Man, we are assured, is descended from ape-like ancestors, moulded by circumstances into men, and these apes again were derived from ancestral forms of a lower order, and so up from the primordial protoplasmic jelly. Clearly, then, man, unless the order of the universe has come to an end, will undergo further modification in the future, and at last cease to be man, giving rise to some other type of animated being. At once the fascinating question arises, What will this being be?[6]

The essential idea that Wells imbibed from Huxley is that *Homo sapiens* is not the apex of creation but simply a finite species that has emerged after a long process of adaptation and evolution, and that the species will continue to evolve in ways that cannot at present be foreseen. What fascinated him as a student was the question of the form this future evolution would take. His biological studies convinced him that the course of evolution would be far more problematic than the facile assumptions of utopian writers would suggest.

Throughout his student years and the years immediately following, he contributed articles, verse, and stories to the *Science Schools Journal* under a variety of pseudonyms—Walker Glockenhammer, Septimus Browne, Sosthenes Smith, Tyro, and H. G. Wheels—as well as contributions that would be published under his own name.

These pieces include two short stories, "The Devotee of Art" and "Walcote: A Tale of the Twentieth Century," which is a humorous account of the application of a perpetual-motion machine to the London Underground; and "A Vision of the Past," in which the narrator dreams he is in an age of reptilian monsters who are convinced that *they* are the lords of creation and that the world was made for *them*. In later years Wells was inclined to be very disparaging about these early writings; they were, he said, "imitative puerile stuff."[7] But writers can be very unreliable commentators on their own work. Despite his reservations there is much of interest in these early essays and stories. In such pieces as "A Talk with Gryllotalpa" and "A Vision of the Past" there is abundant evidence of the narrative skill and facility with words that was later to stand him in such good stead, and in a story such as "The Devotee of Art" there is ample promise of greater things to come.[8]

After a promising start as a science student he left the college in the summer of 1887 without a degree. In his first year he had found Thomas Henry Huxley an inspiring teacher of biology, but his tutors during his second and third years, Professor Guthrie (physics) and Professor Judd (geology) were lackluster by comparison. Also, he was increasingly distracted by other interests: writing for the *Science Schools*

Journal, meetings of the college Debating Society, and dabbling in the works of Carlyle, Shelley, Blake, and Ruskin. He had moreover become infatuated with his cousin Isabel Mary Wells and spent much time with her when he should have been occupied with his studies.

He celebrated his twenty-first birthday in September 1887 ill in bed at a wretched private school in North Wales known as the Holt Academy, where he was for a short period a schoolmaster. He had been badly fouled while playing soccer and sustained a crushed kidney, the effects of which he would suffer for many years. Despite poor health he remained at Holt from July to November 1887, then traveled to Uppark for a long convalescence. He was by this time suffering from hemorrhages and for some months lived the life of a semi-invalid.

THE IMPACT OF UPPARK

Uppark, the great house on the Sussex Downs where his mother was housekeeper, was by no means typical of country houses of that era. It was a microcosm of an earlier age, frozen in a time warp. Built about 1690, surrounded by walled gardens, a deer park, and undulating countryside, it was remote from urbanity or any intrusive influence. Due to an accident of history, the interior of Uppark had hardly changed for a century or more. Two widowed sisters lived in the house in a world of attenuated ritual, a world in which nothing changed from decade to decade, and where the prevailing tone was one of Dickens's *Bleak House*. House parties, shooting, hunting, balls, and dinners formed the substance of its life. The young Wells, observing this upstairs/downstairs world with irreverent detachment, must have been struck by the contrast between this and society outside, and noted how gently yet inevitably the hand of change rested upon it. Later, in his novel *Tono-Bungay*, he was to give a striking picture of Uppark in the guise of Bladesover House, using the rise and fall of the country house as a metaphor for the decline and breakup of the Victorian age.

The house possessed a fine eclectic library, into which Wells as a boy and as a young man was allowed to dip freely. Here he encountered Swift's *Gulliver's Travels*, Voltaire's *Candide*, Johnson's *Rasselas*, and Beckford's *Vathek*. These romances awakened him to the notion that the hierarchical society he saw all about him in the great house was not immutable and that there were possible ways of living utterly removed from the everyday world. This idea was strengthened by his reading of Plato's *Republic*, in which he encountered for the first time the concept of an ideal state. Swift and Voltaire made a significant impact on the young Wells, for from these authors he derived the notion of describing an *imaginary* world as a means of satirizing the real world. The seed of this idea was firmly planted in his mind and came to fruition in *The Time Machine* and *The Island of Doctor Moreau*.

It would be difficult to exaggerate the impact of Uppark on Wells's imagination; indeed, it would not be too much to say that it was the greatest single influence on his early life. The great house with its deer park and woodlands, its library and paintings, its air of leisured civilization, affected him enormously and played a considerable part in stimulating his imagination. "For me at any rate," he wrote, "the house at Uppark was alive and potent. The place had a great effect on me; it retained a vitality that altogether overshadowed the insignificant ebbing trickle of upstairs life."[9] The house also made a deep impression on him because of its rigid hierarchical structure of staff and servants, and the sharp contrast between life above and below stairs. In the basement are a series of underground passages constructed in 1810 to link the kitchen with the service stairs. These tunnels are ventilated by deep shafts letting in light from the surface. As a boy he would have been very familiar with this system of tunnels and may well have derived the idea of the Morlocks, with their underground passages, from this eerie below-stairs world.

Later he was to portray Uppark as not only Bladesover House in *Tono-Bungay* but Burnmore Park in *The Passionate Friends* and Mowbray in *The World of William Clissold*. Its effect on a youth who had spent all his life in Bromley had the force of a revelation. It awakened him to the importance of social relationships and led him to speculate about the country house and its role in English history. Throughout his mother's tenure as housekeeper he spent many of his holidays at the house, familiarizing himself more and more with its library and slowly modifying his first uncritical impressions. He wrote in *Tono-Bungay* that he was glad he had seen so much of Uppark because "Seeing it when I did, quite naively, believing in it thoroughly, and then coming to analyse it, has enabled me to understand much that would be absolutely incomprehensible in the structure of English society. . . . [I]t is one of those dominant explanatory impressions that make the framework of my mind."[10]

EARLY WRITINGS

Following his convalescence at Uppark he decided to accept an invitation from his friend William Burton to spend some months at his home in the Staffordshire Potteries. From April to July 1888 he stayed with Burton at Etruria (Burton had been a fellow student at South

Kensington). All these experiences—his sojourn in North Wales, his convalescence at Uppark, and his stay in the Potteries—had deep impacts upon him, for throughout this time he was reading and writing voraciously and gaining valuable experience in expressing his thoughts and ideas in essays, verse, and short stories.

His literary efforts continued, and a number of short stories were written at this time. None of these has seen the light of day, and we know that some of them were burned by Wells himself. Writing from Etruria to an old student friend he commented, "Some day I shall succeed, I really believe, but it is a weary game."[11] He had strong literary ambitions and was determined that one day he would be a professional writer. A number of novels were commenced during this period, one of them, *Lady Frankland's Companion,* was presumably based on his impressions of genteel life at Uppark, while another was a sensational melodrama of Five Towns life, strongly influenced by the works of Dostoevsky and Eugene Sue. The latter was subsequently destroyed, with the exception of one fragment that survives as a short story, "The Cone," published in 1895.

The significant points about all these early literary efforts are, first, that throughout this period Wells was gaining increasing self-confidence in self-expression, and, secondly, that he did not give up, however discouraging his continual rejections must have been. He records in his autobiography:

> And at Etruria my real writing began. I produced something as good at least as my letters, something I could read aloud to people I respected without immediate shame. It was good enough to alter and correct and write over again. . . . Moreover I began a romance, very much under the influence of Hawthorne, which was printed in the *Science Schools Journal,* the *Chronic Argonauts.* I broke this off after three instalments because I could not go on with it. That I realised I could not go on with it marks a stage in my education in the art of fiction. It was the original draft of what later became *The Time Machine,* which first won me recognition as an imaginative writer.[12]

We will look more closely at *The Chronic Argonauts* in the "Texts" chapter. It is sufficient to note here that although it is undoubtedly an immature piece of writing, it contains the germ of the idea that eventually came to fruition in *The Time Machine,* for the essence of the story concerns an inventor (quaintly named Nebogipfel) who journeys through time. Unfortunately Wells mars the story with melodramatic touches borrowed from Hawthorne's *The Scarlet Letter;* he wisely decided that he could not complete it in accordance with his original design. It remains a tantalizing fragment, interesting to scholars partly because the early work of a major writer always merits scrutiny, and partly because of its intrinsic importance as the earliest version of his scientific romance. Following its publication in the *Science Schools Journal* he continued to worry away at his idea, for he sensed he had hit on something important and was reluctant to abandon it.

It can be seen that the year 1888 was a crucial one for Wells. His three years as a science student were over, and he badly needed a new direction in life. He was already determined to be a writer and was working hard on a number of literary projects. Although he still had a long apprenticeship ahead of him—it was not until eight years later, in 1895, that *The Time Machine* would be published—his main concerns as a writer were already apparent. He was passionately interested in the future and in speculating on the probable shape of human destiny. He was fascinated by evolution and by the possible course of biological development. Above all, he was aware of his ability to write about ordinary men and women and to depict them in extraordinary situations. This gift of inviting suspension of disbelief was to prove one of his greatest strengths.

There can be no mistaking his determination to be a writer. In May 1889, at the age of twenty-two, he told his brother Fred that he was "writing fitfully at various schemes for stories, though I have been at it for two years or more now, there is yet all to learn in the art of fiction. But, failing death, I mean to learn it, and that learnt, to write and print, to succeed and sell."[13] In July 1891 came his first real breakthrough, with the publication of "The Rediscovery of the Unique" in Frank Harris's influential journal the *Fortnightly Review*. This essay, which Wells described as his "first quarrel with the accepted logic,"[14] postulated the uniqueness of all living things and the error inherent in rigid classifications. Since all individuals are unique, he argued, it follows that there can be no such thing as universally applicable moral laws: "We cannot think of regulating our conduct by wholesale dicta." In its insistence on the provisionality of man and of logical processes and language, "The Rediscovery of the Unique" is characteristic of attitudes he was to hold throughout his life. In place of a confident faith in social advance the essay reveals a profound sense of doubt, a troubled awareness of a universe in which there can be no certainties.

"The neat little picture of a universe of souls made up of passions and principles in bodies made of atoms, all put together so neatly and wound up at the creation, fades in the series of dissolving views that we call the march of human thought."[15]

This sense of a society in process of fragmentation is a frequently recurring theme in his early writings and one to which he returned many times as a mature writer. Though he was greatly elated by Frank Harris's acceptance of the essay, his attempt to follow it up with "The Universe Rigid"—an account of a four-dimensional time-space system—came to nothing, for this was rejected by Harris as unreadable.

Later in the same year, in an essay entitled "Zoological Retrogression," he stressed that there is "no guarantee in scientific knowledge of man's permanence or permanent ascendancy." He continued: "The presumption is that before him lies a long future of profound modification, but whether that will be, according to present ideals, upward or downward, no one can forecast."[16]

This insistence that the future course of evolution might conceivably be one of retrogression rather than advancement was a bold stance for a young writer to take, and one that was diametrically opposed to the fashionable views of the time. It was a stance that preoccupied him more and more as he gained increasing self-confidence as a contributor to educational and scientific journals.

After working for some years as a schoolmaster in London, he became a biology tutor for the University Correspondence College and in October 1891 married his cousin Isabel. The marriage was not a success, for mentally and temperamentally they were ill suited; they parted in January 1894 when Wells eloped with one of his students, Amy Catherine Robbins.

Amy, or "Jane," as H.G. christened her, was much less conventional than Isabel and was willing to throw in her lot with his, even though she knew he was married and in poor health. She too was not strong but became utterly devoted to Wells and determined to encourage him in his literary ambitions. Small, fragile, and delicate, she clung to him with steadfast loyalty. Aspects of her personality are reflected in the figure of Weena, the girl whom the Time Traveler rescues from drowning. Though in real life Jane was a determined person, in contrast to the rather indolent Weena, there are echoes of her character in the childlike devotion with which Weena attaches herself to the Traveler. Jane became Wells's constant companion and helpmate, and stuck to him through thick and thin. They married as soon as he was free to do so.

Throughout this period he devoted all his spare time to writing until a breakdown in his health in the summer of 1893 forced him to abandon teaching as a career and concentrate all his energies on journalism. From August 1893 onward a steady stream of articles and essays began to appear, principally in the *Pall Mall Gazette*. These essays, many of which were collected in *Select Conversations with an Uncle* (1895) and *Certain Personal Matters* (1897), range widely over everyday themes but also include articles on scientific topics. Of the latter the most significant are "The Man of the Year Million" and "The Extinction of Man." In "The Man of the Year Million" he asserts that "evolution is no mechanical tendency making for perfection. . . . [I]t is simply the continual adaptation of plastic life, for good or evil, to the circumstances that surround it." "The Extinction of Man" elaborates this theme, arguing that "in no case does the record of the fossils show a really dominant species succeeded by its own descendants" and concluding with the assertion that "man's complacent assumption of the future is too confident."[17] These essays implicitly challenge the notion that evolution must inevitably lead to progress, and they run counter to much optimistic writing of the time.

Early in 1894 he was invited by W. E. Henley, the editor of the *National Observer*, to write a series of articles for the magazine. Wells accepted at once, recording later in his autobiography:

> I resolved to do my very best for him and I dug up my peculiar treasure, my old idea of "time-travelling" from the *Science Schools Journal* and sent him in a couple of papers. He liked them and asked me to carry on the idea so as to give glimpses of the world of the future. This I was only too pleased to do, and altogether I developed the notion into seven papers between March and June.[18]

When later the *National Observer* ceased publication, Henley launched a new journal, *The New Review*, and invited Wells to be among the contributors. He readily agreed, rewriting the time-traveling articles that had been published in the *National Observer* under the title "The Time Traveller's Story" and reshaping them as a gripping narrative. Not only was this accepted for serial publication, but Heinemann agreed to publish it as a book. With the publication of this, his first novel, at the age of twenty-eight, he was firmly launched on a literary career.

The Time Machine thus represents a fusion of ideas that had preoccupied Wells through much of his early life. Darwin's theory of evolution had opened up a range of speculations concerning the future course of human development. Coupled with this was Wells's intense curiosity regarding society, stimulated by his observations of English life as he had seen it at Bromley and at Uppark. This in turn was linked in his mind with the ideas of Plato and the suggestion that "the whole fabric of law, custom and worship, which seemed so invincibly established, might be cast into the melting pot and made anew."[19] Allied to all these ideas was his biological training, his secular view of the world, and his critical approach to many of the accepted orthodoxies of his time. The young Wells, turning over these considerations in his mind, seized on the concept of time travel as the key to his vision. It is little wonder that he described it as his "peculiar treasure" and that it was his *idée fixe* during the years 1888–94, when he was working on draft after draft of his story.

THE NOVELIST AS PROPHET

In an interview published in 1899, when he was a rising young author, Wells was asked the question, "What is your object in dealing with the men and women of the future instead of utilising men and women as they exist now?" He replied:

> I have a special object in doing that. I am strongly of opinion that we ought to consider the possibilities of the future much more than we do. Why should four-fifths of the fiction of today be concerned with times that can never come again, while the future is scarcely speculated upon? At present we are almost helpless in the grip of circumstances, and I think we ought to strive to shape our destinies. Changes that directly affect the human race are taking place every day, but they are passed over unobserved.[20]

The phrase *strive to shape our destinies* is significant and points to Wells's motives in so much of his work. From *The Time Machine* onward much of his fiction takes the form of an imaginative account of a possible society, implicitly contrasted with the world of the present. This is evident in such works as *When the Sleeper Wakes* (1899), *The First Men in the Moon* (1901), *The Food of the Gods* (1904), *A Modern Utopia* (1905), *Men Like Gods* (1923), and *Mr. Blettsworthy on Rampole Island* (1928). Much of his work is an implied criticism of the world as it is, employing satire, irony, and invective to achieve his effects. He described the last of his dystopias, *Mr. Blettsworthy on Rampole Island,* as "a caricature-portrait of the whole human world."[21]

He was surely right to remind his readers that "changes which directly affect the human race are taking place every day." The first twenty-one years of his own life had been notable for an explosion of scientific innovation, including the invention of the internal combustion engine, the typewriter, the telephone, the electric railway, electric street lighting, the gramophone, the box camera, and color photography. These years had also seen the publication of Darwin's *The Descent of Man,* the coining of the word "agnostic" (by Wells's teacher T. H. Huxley), and an unprecedented ferment of debate concerning man's place in the universe.

It is difficult for a twenty-first-century reader to imagine the impact this climate of change must have had on Wells's mind. He had been brought up in a world in which all seemed immutable. Queen Victoria had been on the throne since 1837, ruling over an empire that seemed destined to endure for eternity. His mother had taught him to respect his "elders and betters," not to question authority, and to resign himself to accept his lot in life. He would write of her: "Her mind was fixed and definite, she embodied all that confidence in church and decorum and the assurances of the pulpit which was characteristic of the large mass of the English people . . . in early Victorian times."[22] His own mind, in complete contrast, was neither fixed nor definite. It was a mind receptive to new ideas, eager to embrace and assimilate the world of science, discovery, and thought.

Given this background it is not surprising that from the outset metamorphosis was the leading motif of his fiction. It is not simply that he was fascinated by the teeming possibilities of science and discovery, though there is ample evidence in such stories as "The Argonauts of the Air," "Filmer," and "The Land Ironclads" that he was deeply interested in the potentialities of human ingenuity. What interested him much more was the way in which life can be *changed* by apparently random events. Some of his most memorable tales—"The Man Who Could Work Miracles," "A Slip under the Microscope," "Aepyornis Island," "The Story of the Late Mr. Elvesham"—hinge on the idea of metamorphosis, of the transformation of an individual as a result of an unpredicted occurrence. The dominating idea of his fiction is *flux*—the notion that life is not static but fluid, infinitely variable. Complacency and predictability are his targets: "We think that we shall always go to work at ten and leave off at four and have dinner at seven for ever and ever."[23] The importance of hazard in human affairs cannot be overemphasized, he argues. No one can foresee what encounter or what twist of fate lies just beyond the horizon; the most hidebound life can be changed beyond recognition by a discovery, a meeting, or an accident.

The idea of the malleability of life was central to his conception of the role of fiction. To Wells the function of the novel was to stimulate thought, to suggest possibilities of behavior and experience that would enlarge the frontiers of everyday living. As the nineteenth century moved to its close, more and more writers seized on the idea of change as a fruitful source of conjecture. What would the new century bring? What would be the probable shape of things to come? Wells was one of the first writers of his generation to embrace the idea of change, not simply because he sensed that change was part of the spirit of the age but because he knew in his innermost self that life, both for mankind as a whole and for the individual, could not remain static. His most enduring contribution to the novel as a genre is the ease with which he communicates to the reader a sense of life as a panorama teeming with possibilities. In his hands all seems possible, nothing seems definite. In his world nothing can be taken for granted.

WELLS'S LITERARY REPUTATION

Today Wells belongs to literary history. He is remembered for the brilliant series of scientific romances beginning with *The Time Machine,* for his "realistic" novels in the manner of Dickens, and for his short stories. He is also remembered as a popular educator, the author of *The Outline of History* and *A Short History of the World,* and a man who campaigned tirelessly for human betterment. Yet today, sixty years after his death, critics remain deeply divided as to his literary standing.

His famous quarrel with Henry James concerning the means and ends of literature has done untold damage to his literary reputation, partly because it has led to the misconception that he did not care about the quality of his work, and partly because there is a widespread impression that James got the better of the argument. But as Robert Bloom has demonstrated in his *Anatomies of Egotism,* the debate is still going on, and it is by no means certain that James was the victor.[24] Wells summarized their debate in these terms:

> The important point which I tried to argue with Henry James was that the novel of completely consistent characterization arranged beautifully in a story and painted deep and round and solid, no more exhausts the possibilities of the novel than the art of Velázquez exhausts the possibilities of the painted picture. The issue exercised my mind considerably. I had a queer feeling that we were both incompatibly right.[25]

What is certainly true is that Wells did himself a disservice by belittling his own status as a novelist. At the height of their quarrel he was stung into declaring, "I had rather be called a journalist than an artist, that is the essence of it."[26]

The legend persists that he was a facile writer who rarely took pains over his work. In fact, the reverse is the case. The manuscripts of most of his novels and short stories still survive—they are preserved at the University of Illinois at Urbana-Champaign, which acquired them after his death. The manuscripts are all written in his minute spidery handwriting (no word processors in those days). These reveal that his stories were most carefully written and revised, often going through draft after draft before reaching their final version. "A Dream of Armageddon," for example, went through six versions before he was satisfied, and the different drafts of "The Country of the Blind" reveal an extraordinary degree of indecision, particularly over its final paragraph.

We now know far more about his methods of work than was apparent during his lifetime. His holograph manuscripts are available to scholars, and his letters to his literary friends, especially those to Arnold Bennett and George Gissing, have been published. These reveal that he cared deeply about his literary reputation and took immense pains to revise and reshape his work.

Bernard Loing, in his seminal study *H. G. Wells at Work,* has demonstrated that Wells was a conscious and deliberate literary artist, and this is confirmed by the studies of other Wells scholars, including Bernard Bergonzi, Harris Wilson, William Scheick, and Robert Philmus.[27] Despite his protestations that he was a journalist, the fact remains that with few exceptions, his fiction was composed with elaborate care and that he was a compulsive reviser of his own work. He was still "tinkering" with the text of *The Time Machine* until well into the twentieth century.

IS TIME TRAVEL POSSIBLE?

The idea of time travel, which has become a commonplace of science fiction, received a considerable stimulus with the publication of *The Time Machine.* Wells himself returned to it in his short story "The New Accelerator" (1901), in which a scientist discovers a drug that accelerates the speed of the body thousands of times beyond normal. The narrator observes that the discovery "is the beginning of our escape from that Time Garment of which Carlyle speaks." The notion of journeying through time into a different age—or, as the Time Traveler expresses it, "slipping like a vapour through the interstices of intervening substances"—has exercised a potent appeal for generations of science fiction writers and is the staple of such films as *Doctor Who* and *Back to the Future*. In 1988 Britain's leading cosmic physicist, Stephen Hawking, argued in his *A Brief History of Time* that time travel was contrary to the laws of physics. Human beings, he asserted, had to come to terms with the present; there was no way out. A time machine would warp space-time so severely that human beings would be destroyed.

However, this view has been challenged by other scientists, including Dr. Amos Ori of Israel and the British quantum physicist Dr. David Deutsch. Those who dissent from Hawking's theories argue that black holes could provide gateways through time and that the universe should be seen as a "multiverse" in which all possible histories happen simultaneously. According to this argument Einstein's general theory of relativity (published in 1916) demonstrated that gravity warps the fabric of space-time. The same theory also asserted that under certain circumstances, such as inside a rotating black hole, the warping becomes so severe that space-time is torn and folded back on itself, providing pathways into the past. While, according to this theory, travel into the *past* may be theoretically possible, however, there remain serious arguments against the possibility of travel into the *future*. The debate among quantum physicists will undoubtedly continue. What can be said with certainty is that the concept of journeying backward or forward in time and thus escaping from one's own age is one of the most fruitful concepts in literature and that in launching the Time Traveler on his journey Wells was starting more than he knew. As we speculate on the idea of time travel we see again the young H. G. Wells toiling away on the manuscript of *The Chronic Argonauts,* his imagination fired by "the ship that sails through time" and dreaming of his hero who proclaims "and now I go to join my generation, to journey through the ages till my time has come."

A STORY FOR ALL TIME

One can only speculate what Wells's reaction would have been to the news that in August 1989 Uppark, the great house in which he had spent so much of his boyhood and adolescence, was badly damaged by fire. For a time, at the height of the inferno, it appeared that the house had been gutted and would have to be demolished. When the flames had subsided it was apparent that though the attic and upper story had been destroyed, the remainder of the house, with its priceless contents, had survived largely intact. The National Trust took the courageous decision to restore the house to its former glory; the house was reopened to the public in the summer of 1995.

Thus, exactly a hundred years after the publication of *The Time Machine,* the house that influenced Wells so much, and the tunnels of which may have provided the inspiration for the underground passages of the Morlocks, rose like a phoenix from the ashes. There is a strange irony in the fact that the house that to the young Wells seemed frozen in a time warp—but that he described as "alive and potent"—should have proven so resilient. *Non omnis moriar,* a quotation from Horace, is the motto of the Fetherstonhaugh family who have lived at Uppark for centuries. It means, roughly translated, "I shall not wholly die." Both the house and the novel engendered in its shadow will go on to be enjoyed by generations yet to come.

More than a century has now elapsed since the first publication of *The Time Machine* in book form. The book continues to be read in a wide variety of editions and languages. Each year sees a new generation of readers approaching the novel for the first time; each year brings a fresh crop of critical essays discussing aspects of the narrative—its structure, symbolism, interpretation and mythos. What are the reasons for its continuing popularity? How are we to account for the fact that a first novel written by a hitherto little-known writer has achieved canonical status?

In the chapters that follow we will look at these questions more closely. What is certain is that *The Time Machine* shows no signs of losing its popularity. It goes on from strength to strength, carrying Wells's name onward into that literary immortality he affected to shun.

NOTES

1. Wells, introduction to volume 1, *The Atlantic Edition of the Works of H. G. Wells* (London: Fisher Unwin, and New York: Charles Scribners, 1924), ix–xx.
2. Wells, *The Desert Daisy* (Urbana, Ill.: Beta Phi Mu, 1957).
3. Wells, *Textbook of Biology* (London: University Correspondence College, 1893), 131.
4. E. A. Hamilton-Gordon, "The Fourth Dimension," *Science Schools Journal* (April 1887): 145–51.
5. Wells, preface to *The Time Machine* (New York: Random House, 1931), viii.
6. Wells, "The Man of the Year Million," *Pall Mall Gazette,* 6 November 1893, 3. This essay is reprinted in *Certain Personal Matters* under the title "Of a Book Unwritten."
7. Quoted in Geoffrey West, *H. G. Wells: A Sketch for a Portrait* (London: Howe, 1930), 287.
8. "The Devotee of Art" and "Walcote" are included in John Hammond, ed., *The Complete Short Stories of H. G. Wells* (London: Dent, 1998). "A Vision of the Past" and "A Talk with Gryllotalpa" are included in Robert Philmus

and David Y. Hughes, eds., *H. G. Wells: Early Writings in Science and Science Fiction* (Berkeley: University of California Press, 1975).

9. Wells, *Experiment in Autobiography* (London: Gollancz, 1934), 137.

10. Wells, *Tono-Bungay* (London: Macmillan, 1909), book 1, chap. 1.

11. Wells, letter to A. M. Davies, May 1888. A collected edition of Wells's letters is David Smith, ed., *The Correspondence of H. G. Wells* (London: Pickering and Chatto, 1998), four volumes.

12. Wells, *Experiment in Autobiography,* 309.

13. Letter to Fred Wells, 28 May 1889. See note 11 above.

14. Wells, "Scepticism of the Instrument," appendix to *A Modern Utopia* (London: Chapman and Hall, 1905), 378.

15. Wells, "The Rediscovery of the Unique," *Fortnightly Review* (July 1891): 106–11. Reprinted in Philmus and Hughes, eds., *H. G. Wells: Early Writings in Science and Science Fiction,* 22–31.

16. Wells, "Zoological Retrogression," *Gentleman's Magazine* (September 1891): 246–53. Reprinted in Philmus and Hughes, eds., *H. G. Wells: Early Writings in Science and Science Fiction,* 158–68.

17. Wells, "The Man of the Year Million," *Pall Mall Gazette*, 6 November 1893 (see note 6 above); "The Extinction of Man," *Pall Mall Gazette,* 25 September 1894, reprinted in *Certain Personal Matters.*

18. Wells, *Experiment in Autobiography,* 515–16.

19. Ibid., 138.

20. "The Novelist as Prophet," *Cassell's Saturday Journal,* 26 April 1899.

21. Wells, *Experiment in Autobiography,* 501.

22. Wells, *The New Machiavelli* (London: Bodley Head, 1911), book 1, chap. 3. This comment is widely recognized as autobiographical.

23. Wells, "The Extinction of Man" (see note 17 above).

24. Robert Bloom, *Anatomies of Egotism: A Reading of the Last Novels of H. G. Wells* (Lincoln: University of Nebraska Press, 1977), 9–38. See also J. R. Hammond, *H. G. Wells and the Modern Novel* (London: Macmillan, 1988), 24–41.

25. Wells, *Experiment in Autobiography,* 493.

26. Wells, letter to Henry James, 8 July 1915.

27. Cf. Bernard Loing, *H. G. Wells at Work* (Paris: Didier Erudition, 1984). See also Bernard Bergonzi, *The Early H. G. Wells* (Manchester: Manchester University Press, 1961); Harris Wilson, ed., *The Wealth of Mr Waddy* (Carbondale: Southern Illinois University Press, 1969); William Scheick, *The Splintering Frame: The Later Fiction of H. G. Wells* (Victoria, B.C.: University of Victoria, 1984); and Philmus and Hughes, eds., *H. G. Wells: Early Writings in Science and Science Fiction.*

2

Content

In the original edition of *The Time Machine*, published by Heinemann in 1895, the text was divided into sixteen chapters, and each chapter was given a title. When Wells revised his novels for a collected edition in 1924, the Atlantic Edition, he retained the text of *The Time Machine* virtually unaltered but reduced the number of chapters from 16 to 12, eliminating the chapter titles.

Most modern editions follow Wells's revision in dividing the text into twelve chapters. In the discussion that follows chapter references follow this practice.

A comparison of the chapter divisions is as follows:

Heinemann		*Atlantic*
1	Introduction	1
2	The Machine	1
3	The Time Traveller Returns	2
4	Time Travelling	3
5	In the Golden Age	4
6	The Sunset of Mankind	4
7	A Sudden Shock	5
8	Explanation	5
9	The Morlocks	6
10	When the Night Came	7
11	The Palace of Green Porcelain	8
12	In the Darkness	9

Heinemann	*Atlantic*	
13	The Trap of the White Sphinx	10
14	The Further Vision	11
15	The Time Traveller's Return	12
16	After the Story	12
	Epilogue	Epilogue

Chapter 1 of *The Time Machine* opens with a description of a group of friends engaged in conversation at the home of the Time Traveler, who is not named. We learn that the friends meet every Thursday in the Time Traveler's home at Richmond, Surrey, for dinner and conversation. In addition to the Time Traveler, six people are present: the Psychologist, Filby, the Very Young Man, the Provincial Mayor, the Medical Man, and the narrator himself. We are not explicitly told the narrator's name, though it can be inferred from a reference in chapter 12 that his surname is Hillyer.

The opening paragraph at once creates an atmosphere designed to suspend disbelief. The friends have dined well, they are seated in comfortable chairs, and "there was that luxurious after-dinner atmosphere when thought runs gracefully free of the trammels of precision." All is solid, safe, and reassuring. The description of the comfortable room with its warm fire and pleasant ambience ("Our chairs, being his patents, embraced and caressed us rather than submitted to be sat upon") establishes an atmosphere of reality and normality as an introduction to the narrative that is to follow.

This description of the room at Richmond, so carefully written by Wells, is deliberately designed to achieve this effect. He wrote later: "I had realised that the more impossible the story I had to tell, the more ordinary must be the setting, and the circumstances in which I now set the Time Traveller were all that I could imagine of solid upper-middle-class comfort."[1] It is a *framing device* in which an apparently fantastic narrative is placed within a descriptive frame of reassuring familiarity. This device is frequently employed in the nineteenth century novel, and Wells was writing in that respect within a long-established literary tradition.

In this opening chapter the Time Traveler is expounding his theory that time is the fourth dimension. His audience is skeptical, and the Traveler adopts the Socratic method of exposition through question and answer. Each of the friends in turn raises objections to the Traveler's ideas, who is then obliged to clarify and restate his theories. The essence of his argument is that length, breadth, thickness, and *duration* are the four dimensions and that it should be theoretically possible to travel in time as well as through space. He claims to have invented a machine that will travel "in any direction of Space and Time, as the driver determines."

In his book *The Modern Short Story,* H. E. Bates refers to Wells's "charm" as a writer, adding that this charm "will, at some future date, give Wells an attractive touch of period bloom."[2] This period quality is already evident in *The Time Machine*. There are several references to coal fires, a form of heating that was commonplace in England until around 1950. The references to flying seem to a modern reader quaintly out of date; the reader has to make a conscious effort to recall that the story was written in 1894, long before the invention of the airplane. There is a reference to a lecture at the New York Mathematical Society "only a month or so ago"; in fact, this lecture took place in December 1893. When *The Time Machine* was serialized in the *National Observer,* the present chapter 1 appeared in March 1894. We may infer therefore that the after-dinner conversation at Richmond takes place in the early months of 1894.

Following the discussion with his skeptical audience, the Traveler claims to have "experimental verification" and shows them a model Time Machine, about the size of an alarm clock. After giving them an opportunity to examine the model and satisfy themselves there is no trickery, the Traveler then asks the Psychologist to launch the model Machine on a journey through time. Seeing that his friends are still doubtful, the Traveler then invites them to follow him into his laboratory, where he shows them a full-sized Time Machine, not yet complete. "Upon that machine," he proclaims, "I intend to explore time."

In the description of both the model and the full-sized machine there is a contrast between the solid and the unreal. The model contains metal and ivory, yet "there is an odd twinkling appearance about this bar, as though it was in some way unreal." Similarly, the large machine appears to be solid enough—"Parts were of nickel, parts of ivory, parts had certainly been filed or sawn out of rock crystal." Yet when the narrator touches it later in the story "the squat substantial looking mass swayed like a bough shaken by the wind" (89).

The Time Traveler himself is also described in ambiguous terms. The narrator describes his "queer, broad head in silhouette," but as the friends follow him into the laboratory there is a reference to "the flickering light" and "the dance of the shadows." His house, room, and laboratory are solid and real enough, but whether the Traveler is all he appears to be is open to question. The Medical Man and Filby are still inclined to doubt the Traveler's claims, while the narrator himself is noncommittal.

Throughout this introductory chapter Wells is at pains to create the *illusion* of reality. The illusion is achieved through an accumulation of reassuring detail: the comfortable room, the common-sensical audience, the disappearance of the model when trickery seems impossible, the convincing tone of the Traveler, the reality of the Machine. Wells has skilfully prepared the reader for what is to follow.

Chapter 2 opens with a reiteration of the skeptical tone established at the outset: "I think that at that time none of us quite believed in the Time Machine." The narrator explains that the Time Traveler was "one of those men who are too clever to be believed," adding that his friends distrusted him because of his formidable intellectual powers. The narrator and the Medical Man are now inclined to believe that the disappearance of the model was not genuine but an ingenious conjuring trick.

The Psychologist, the Medical Man, and Hillyer meet again for dinner at the Traveler's home on the following Thursday. This time they are joined by three new guests: the Editor of a daily newspaper, a Journalist, and a quiet, shy figure who is referred to as "the Silent Man." They receive a message that the Traveler has been unavoidably detained and that they are to commence dinner without him. The Psychologist explains to the Editor all that has occurred on the previous Thursday; in the midst of his explanation the Traveler silently enters the room, limping and disheveled. He has clearly undergone intense suffering and has a half-healed wound on his face. The Traveler explains that he is "starving for a bit of meat" and that he will wash and change and then join his guests at the dinner table.

While the Traveler is absent from the room the guests speculate as to whether he has been time traveling and why he is looking so unkempt. The Editor is incredulous but announces he will "give a shilling a line for a verbatim note."

The Traveler takes his place at the table and eats voraciously. Having eaten, he apologizes for his apparent bad manners but adds that he was extremely hungry and has had some amazing experiences. He then invites his guests to accompany him into the smoking room and promises to relate the full story of his adventures, on condition that they do not interrupt him. He has lived "such days as no human being ever lived before." His friends agree not to interrupt him, and he forthwith launches into his narrative.

The whole of this second chapter is a continuation of the framing device commenced in chapter 1. It reinforces the background of a known, familiar world: the group of respectable people who meet every week, the detail of the meal (they are eating mutton), the conversation over dinner, the description of the Traveler, the circumstantial account of his arrival, and the careful way in which the scene is set for his storytelling. Wells adds a final touch to enhance the realism of the scene and increase the reader's suspense: "You will read, I will suppose, attentively enough; but you cannot see the speaker's white, sincere face in the bright circle of the little lamp, nor hear the intonation of his voice." The narrator is addressing the reader directly and inviting him to become a member of the audience. From this point onward you, the reader, are drawn irresistibly into the circle of listeners.

The Time Traveler's account of his sojourn in the year 802,701 forms the substance of chapters 3 to 11. The third chapter begins with a detailed description of the experience of time traveling—a sensation he describes as "excessively unpleasant." He vividly conveys the sense of helpless, headlong motion, the feeling of trepidation, the fear of an imminent collision. He is traveling through time at such a speed that the landscape appears to be a blur: "The whole surface of the earth seemed changed—melting and flowing under my eyes." At last the feeling of prolonged falling becomes unbearable, but instead of slowing down gradually and coming to a gentle stop (as would surely have been wiser) he stops the machine suddenly and is "flung headlong through the air."

There then follows a description of his arrival in the future, a passage—left virtually unaltered from the earliest drafts—that must be one of the most celebrated paragraphs in the history of science fiction:

> There was the sound of a clap of thunder in my ears. I may have been stunned for a moment. A pitiless hail was hissing round me, and I was sitting on soft turf in front of the overset machine. Everything still seemed grey, but presently I remarked that the confusion in my ears was gone. I looked round me. I was on what seemed to be a little lawn in a garden, surrounded by rhododendron bushes, and I noticed that their mauve and purple blossoms were dropping in a shower under the beating of the hail-stones. The rebounding, dancing hail hung in a cloud over the machine, and drove along the ground like smoke. In a moment I was wet to the skin. "Fine hospitality," said I, "to a man who has travelled innumerable years to see you" (21).

Note the literary touches that heighten the dramatic quality of the scene: the clap of thunder, the pitiless hail, the sense of being concussed, the greyness, the falling blossoms. The fact that he has arrived on a lawn enclosed by bushes enhances the sense of drama implicit in the scene. In his study *The Machine in the Garden,* Leo Marx states: "The sudden appearance of the machine in the garden is an arresting, endlessly evocative image. It causes the instantaneous clash of opposed states of mind."[3] It is indeed a striking image: the Time Machine represents science, technology and learning. The garden represents beauty, the pastoral ideal and the aesthetic virtues. The apposition of classical and romantic in this sudden juxtaposition is a powerful symbol characteristic of Wells.

The Traveler becomes aware that he is standing not far from a large statue of a winged sphinx, carved of white marble. This enigmatic figure, "greatly weather-worn," fascinates him, and he studies it for some time, watching it appear to advance and recede through the mists of the hailstorm.

Doubts then begin to assail him. Is his journey into futurity a wise idea after all? What if humanity has developed in ways he has not foreseen? What if *Homo sapiens* has degenerated into a malign species to whom he might appear to be a savage, a primitive creature "to be incontinently slain"? For the first time in chapter 3 we are given an insight into the Traveler's temperament. Hitherto he has been portrayed as a dispassionate man of science—an intellectual driven solely by the quest for knowledge. Now it becomes apparent that he is also prey to irrational drives. He is aware of "a kind of madness growing upon me," he takes foolish risks, he feels the normal human emotions of anger, fear, petulance, and dread. The Traveler remains a man of science, but he is also revealed as a fallible human being.

The chapter closes with his first encounter with the Eloi, "a group of figures clad in rich soft robes." These graceful, attractive, but frail people approach the Traveler without fear, surrounding him and his machine. Their appearance of fragility and lack of aggression inspires him with confidence. Losing his temerity at having journeyed into an unknown future, he takes his hands from the machine and faces them boldly.

His attempts to converse with these little people forms the opening of chapter 4. The Traveler finds the Eloi gentle and graceful but extremely feeble. Fearing that they may accidentally set the Time Machine in motion by interfering with the levers that control it, he removes the levers and places them in his pocket. The Eloi appear to be inoffensive but lacking in initiative or curiosity. He likens his attempts to converse with them to trying to talk to small children. Presently one of the Eloi places a chain of flowers round his neck, and the others follow suit. He is soon covered in blossom and beautiful flowers.

The Eloi then lead the Traveler to a nearby building, "a vast grey edifice of fretted stone." Leaving the Time Machine behind him on the lawn, the Traveler follows the little people into a great hall. Here the Eloi seat themselves at stone tables and proceed to eat fruit; he soon follows their example, as he is hungry and thirsty. While eating he attempts to understand something of their language but finds it hard work, as they soon tire and derive amusement from his efforts to pronounce their words. At length, his hunger satisfied, he wearies of his efforts at conversation and wanders out of the hall alone. He is struck by the ruinous appearance of all around him: the derelict remains of once-splendid buildings, the curtains thick with dust, the pervading air of decay. He sits down on a seat on the crest of a hill and surveys the surrounding landscape. He forms the conclusion that humanity is on the wane (this chapter was originally entitled "The Sunset of Mankind") and speculates that advancing material progress has been accompanied by a decline in curiosity and enterprise. It seems to him that with no danger of war or disease, no natural predators, and no necessity for innovation, humanity has declined into a state of indolence; humanity has subsided into "languor and decay." He convinces himself that this is the explanation for all he has seen so far. He is satisfied that this theory will account for the abandoned ruins and for the apparent passivity of the Eloi; he has happened to arrive in the future at a point when the human race is declining toward inactivity and extinction. But he then adds a warning to the reader: "Very simple was my explanation, and plausible enough—as most wrong theories are!"

Chapter 5, the longest chapter in *The Time Machine*, is filled with incident and begins with a moment of high drama. The Time Traveler surveys the scene before him, his eyes focusing on the White Sphinx and the little lawn with the rhododendron bushes. At first he thinks he must be mistaken, because he cannot see the Time Machine. The sense of being marooned in the world of 802,701 and never being able to return to his own age grips him with the force of a physical sensation: "At once, like a lash across the face, came the possibility of losing my own age, of being left helpless in this strange new world." When Wells came to write his autobiography forty years later, he still vividly recalled composing this part of the narrative.[4]

In a panic of fear and dread, the Traveler runs from the hill crest to the lawn, cursing his folly in leaving the machine untended. He is convinced the Eloi could not have moved it, as they are physically too feeble. He is also certain it cannot have moved in time, as he still has the levers in his pocket. He searches in vain for the machine, sobbing and raving, and pleading with the little people to explain its whereabouts. Feeling alone and wretched, he lies down on the ground near the sphinx and falls asleep in the open.

Awakening the following morning, he is filled with a sense of despair and frustration. Gradually the anger of the previous day is replaced by a more reasoned mood. He sees the futility of losing his temper with the Eloi and realizes that if he is to regain possession of the machine he must be calm and patient, using his resources of intelligence and guile to learn the ways of the new world so that eventually a new machine can be built. After a careful examination of the lawn and of the sphinx, however, he concludes that the pedestal of the sphinx is hollow and that the machine is inside it. Strange narrow footprints are on the lawn, and grooves are evident where the machine has been moved. But by whom?

The Traveler then resumes his explorations of the surrounding area—"Yet a certain feeling, you may understand, tethered me in a circle of a few miles round the point of my arrival." He resumes his attempts to understand the language of the Eloi and concludes that the language is far simpler than he had at first thought.

He notices a number of circular wells, each protected by a cupola from the rain. Each well seems to be of great depth, and the thudding of machinery can be heard arising from them. He realizes how little he knows of this world and compares his ignorance to that of an African Negro attempting to describe contemporary London. He has by now abandoned his theory of a decadent humanity, as it leaves so much unaccounted for. He has seen no shops, no industry, and no evidence of manufacture, however; he cannot understand the basis of the civilization surrounding him.

At this point his life is transformed in a totally unexpected way. While watching a group of the Eloi bathing in a river he becomes aware that one of them has been seized with a cramp and is drowning. None of the Eloi makes any attempt to rescue her, so he wades in to the river and brings her safely to dry land. During the afternoon of the same day she encounters him again and presents him a garland of flowers in gratitude. They converse, and he learns that her name is Weena. He derives great comfort from this friendship. She is childlike in her devotion to him and wants to follow him everywhere. Hitherto he has been alone and friendless; now at least he has a companion.

From Weena he learns that fear has not left the world and that a dread of the dark is widespread. The little people dread the night and sleep in groups rather than alone. He finds their evident fear of the nighttime puzzling and disturbing.

One moonlit night he sees strange apelike creatures moving in the twilight. They appear to be carrying a body. He is intrigued by this apparition but cannot account for it with a rational explanation. Some time later, on a hot morning, he is exploring a ruined building and is startled to see a pair of eyes watching him out of the darkness. He challenges the creature and again sees an apelike figure disappearing into the shadows. He has the impression of a dull-white creature with large eyes and flaxen hair. The Traveler concludes that these creatures inhabit the underground world below the circular wells.

Musing on this idea, he forms the theory that "Man had not remained one species, but had differentiated into two distinct animals"—the graceful people living above ground and these apelike beings existing below ground. He toys with this idea in his mind and finds it plausible, inferring that it is the below-ground creatures who have moved the Time Machine. Once again, however, he warns the reader that the theory may be wrong. On the face of it he feels that the idea is tenable—that mankind had divided into two distinct species, a subterranean race engaged in manual occupations, the Morlocks; and an above-ground species living in indolence and decline, the Eloi.

But he is still tormented by doubts: Why has the Time Machine been moved? What prevents the Eloi from regaining the machine? Above all, why are the Eloi so afraid of the dark?

The fifth chapter, then, occupies a pivotal role in the narrative. The Traveler loses control of his machine and with it the ability to return to his own age. He has seen Morlocks for the first time and gained some inkling of their place in the scheme of things. He has formed a theory to account for the two distinctive species. Most importantly, he has found a friend, Weena, who provides him with companionship and solace for almost the entire duration of his stay in 802,701.

The following chapter opens with the Traveler resuming his speculations concerning the Morlocks. He regards them with abhorrence and is oppressed with feelings of perplexity and fear. But he feels comforted by Weena's presence and is reassured by the company of the Eloi. He realizes that soon the nights will no longer be moonlit and dreads the coming of darkness. He is also aware that the Time Machine can be regained only by penetrating the deep wells, but he is deterred by the unpleasantness of the task.

Beset with doubt and insecurity he continues his explorations, wandering southward toward Combe Wood and Banstead. In the far distance he sees a vast building apparently faced with green porcelain. Intrigued by this discovery, he resolves to walk to it on the following day, but in his inner self he knows that his desire to explore the palace is merely a device to delay the essential task of descending into the wells. He resolves therefore to go down one of the wells without any further prevarication.

Accompanied by Weena, he starts out early in the morning to one of the nearby wells and to her dismay begins to climb down the shaft.

He descends down the shaft, placing his hands and feet on protruding metal bars. In this way he descends painfully for two hundred yards; he feels cramped, and the thudding sound of machinery grows louder. He has almost decided to turn back when he sees a narrow tunnel leading to a horizontal passage. Swinging himself into this, he lies down to rest.

He is soon aware of soft hands touching his face and strikes a match to frighten the Morlocks. They appear to have no fear of him, apart from their dislike of light. He continues his journey along the passage and finds himself in a large open space like a huge cave. The atmosphere is oppressive, and he is dimly conscious of huge machines and strange shadows. In the center of the cavern is a table set with a meal of meat.

Torn between his desire to learn more of the Morlocks and his revulsion toward all around him, the Traveler realizes how ill equipped he is, for he has not thought to bring a camera or any kind of weapon. His supply of matches is also running low, for he has wasted many of them in startling the Eloi, for whom they are a novelty. He is now surrounded by Morlocks, who attempt to take the matches from him. Sensing his danger, he retreats to the narrow tunnel and tries to escape. The Morlocks are determined to haul him back, and there is a desperate struggle in the darkness, the Traveler frantically trying to begin his ascent. At last he has his hands on the climbing bars and swiftly clambers up the well, still followed by one of his pursuers. The climb seems endless; he feels faint and thinks he is falling down the shaft, but with a great effort he reaches the well mouth and staggers out into the sunlight. He is greeted by the kisses of Weena, then for a time loses consciousness.

Chapter 7 opens with the Traveler taking stock of his position. He is repelled by what he has seen of the Morlocks, whom he regards as "inhuman and malign." At the same time he is dreading the darkness of the new moon and fears the unknown dangers the darkness may bring. He realizes, however, that he possesses advantages the Eloi do not have, as he has the determination to outwit his adversaries through reason and guile. What he needs is a secure fastness where he can sleep without fear, and weapons. Believing that both of these might be found in the Palace of Green Porcelain, he resolves to go there, accompanied by Weena, even though this will mean a walk of eighteen miles. For much of the journey Weena runs at his side, gathering flowers and placing them in his pockets. (At this point in his narrative the Time Traveller empties his pockets and places two withered flowers, resembling white mallows, upon the table.) They journey on through the now deepening twilight, until, seeing that Weena is tiring, he decides to spend the night in the open and resume the journey the next day.

Before sleeping he looks at the Milky Way. The sight of the stars puts his own troubles into perspective. He is humbled by a sense of the vast distances of space and time; he is also depressed by his awareness of the fate of civilization. Then comes a realization of the likely nature of the meat the Morlocks eat, but he dismisses the thought as too horrible.

The next morning the two continue their journey. The Traveler determines to find a weapon of some kind strong enough to fight the Morlocks. At the same time he needs some means of lighting a fire and an implement powerful enough to break open the doors of the White Sphinx and thus retrieve the machine. Weena he has decided to take with him back to his own time. Turning over these thoughts in his mind, he approaches the ruined palace.

The account of his sojourn in the Palace of Green Porcelain and what he finds there forms the substance of chapter 8. As soon as he approaches it he realizes that it is derelict, far gone in decay; only a few fragments of glass remain in the windows, and the green facing is falling away from the walls. Entering through the open main door, he finds himself in a long gallery thick with dust and realizes he is standing in an abandoned museum. Skeletons of extinct animals, including a megatherium and a brontosaurus, lie in the dust, crumbling into decay, and glass cases containing the remains of exhibits line the walls of the gallery. He grasps the truth that the gallery is simply one section of a once-splendid museum and speculates that other rooms may contain materials and exhibits of practical use to him. Wandering from room to room, he is struck by the eerie silence and the layers of dust. There is evidence that the Morlocks have visited the place at some time, as some of the cases have been bodily removed from their positions.

Exploring further, he finds a gallery devoted to minerals and another section devoted to natural history. Another gallery seems to be built into the side of a hill and leads into a thick darkness, where there are traces of Morlock footprints. Finding a gallery of mechanical exhibits, he breaks off a lever from one of the machines, intending to use it as a mace. He then finds a gallery that had once contained books but now only tattered fragments. Here he "moralised upon the futility of all ambition."

At last the Traveler makes a discovery of fundamental importance—in what appears to be a chemistry gallery, in an air-tight case, he finds a box of matches. He tries them and sees they are still in working order. Excited by his find, he performs a dance, to Weena's huge delight.

Soon afterward he makes an equally fortuitous discovery, a block of camphor, which, he recalls burns with a steady flame. He now has a weapon of sorts, matches, and a candle; well satisfied, he continues his explorations in the hope of discovering firearms or explosives that could be of use against the Morlocks. He eventually finds what appear to be two dynamite cartridges, but these prove to be dummies.

It is now late in the evening, and he decides that he and Weena will spend the night in the open, protected from the Morlocks by a fire, and reach the White Sphinx again the next day.

Chapter 9 commences with the two emerging from the palace and embarking on their journey through the gathering dusk. He is uncomfortably aware that lying between them and a place of safety are some dense woods in which Morlocks may be lurking, but he resolves to push on through the forest before resting. Sensing the immediate presence of Morlocks, he sets fire to some branches in the hope that the flames will cover his retreat. He soon realizes the folly of this, as the tinder-dry branches burst into flames, and the fire rapidly spreads.

Pushing on through the dark trees with Weena at his side, he hears the pattering of feet; the Morlocks are closing in on them. He tries to escape by lighting matches and setting fire to the block of camphor, but his pursuers seem determined to encircle him. As Weena appears to be asleep or exhausted he lays her down on the ground and tries to light a bonfire to keep the Morlocks at bay. At length, utterly exhausted himself, he loses consciousness.

He awakes to find his matches missing and no trace of Weena. The fire has spread, and he is in danger of being surrounded by burning trees and undergrowth. He still has his iron bar, and clutching this, he presses on through the wood, seeing Morlocks dazzled by the glare. In the center of the forest is a hillock, where he sits down to rest and think, overcome with bitterness and grief. He concludes that Weena has died in the fire and feels the "intensest wretchedness" at her death. He is alone and angry in an alien world, but he comforts himself by thinking of his friends in Richmond back in his own time.

As he walks on toward the hiding place of the Time Machine, he finds some loose matches in his pocket. He still has the means of frightening his enemies.

In chapter 10 the Traveler's adventures in the year 802,701 are brought to a conclusion. Early in the morning he arrives in the vicinity of the White Sphinx and laughs bitterly at his former self-confidence. His surroundings are the same—the abundant flowers, the splendid buildings, the verdant scenery, the Eloi in their colorful robes—but his conception of the world is now utterly different. He is filled with grief at the fate that has overtaken the human species and reflects that languor and decay are the price paid for a lack of curiosity and initiative. The Elci, he is convinced, will decline into feebleness, preyed upon by the Morlocks. Meditating thus in the warm sunlight, he falls into a doze and, lying down on the turf, has a refreshing sleep.

Waking shortly before sunset, he approaches the Sphinx, clutching his crowbar in one hand. To his surprise he finds the doors beneath the Sphinx are open, revealing the Time Machine inside. Sensing that this may be a trap, he approaches the machine and finds it has been carefully cleaned and oiled. As he is examining it the bronze doors clang shut and he is in darkness. The Morlocks think he is their prisoner, but the Traveler knows he only has to strike a match, attach the levers, and "depart like a ghost." All his calmness disappears, however, when he finds that his matches will not light—they are safety matches and can only be struck on the box.

The Morlocks close in on him. There is a desperate struggle in the darkness, the Traveler frantically trying to attach the levers and the Morlocks attempting to prevent him from escaping. After a furious struggle, he succeeds. The clinging hands fall away from him, and he is launched on a journey into futurity. Once again he experiences the strange sensation of traveling through time—but this time seated uncomfortably on the machine and filled with nausea and confusion.

The eloquent chapter 11, originally entitled "The Further Vision" contains a remarkable description of the earth in the even more distant future—one of Wells's most haunting and evocative visions.

Realizing that he is hurtling into the future at a prodigious pace, the Traveler is puzzled by the steady twilight that broods over the earth. In place of the alternations of night and day an eerie darkness pervades, broken only by the occasional glare of a comet. The earth has apparently come to rest, with one face continuously to the sun. Consumed with curiosity and foreboding, and remembering his earlier foolhardy reversal of motion, he gradually slows down the machine and comes to a gentle halt.

At first the only living thing he sees is a large butterfly circling in the sky. He is on a sloping, desolate beach surrounded by reddish rocks covered with green lichen and vegetation. The sea is gently rising and falling, but he is breathing fast in a rarefied atmosphere. What he had at first assumed to be a rock is moving toward him; he sees to his horror that it is a giant crab. The fearsome crab approaches him with monstrous claws and gleaming eyes. He then sees another crab behind him, menacing him with whiplike antennae. Swiftly he places his hand on the levers and moves himself forward in time.

He journeys on into the future, "in great strides of a thousand years or more, drawn on by the mystery of the earth's fate." He is fascinated to watch the sun growing duller and larger as the solar system moves on to its gradual extinction. At last, thirty million years hence, he stops once more to look around him. The beach now seems lifeless, and he is oppressed by a feeling of bitter coldness. Snow flakes are eddying down, and he sees a fringe of ice on the margin of the sea. The water is red under the sunset.

Darkness closes in on him, and he is assailed by a cold wind. All is still and utterly silent. Snowflakes become more abundant, and the sky becomes inky black. Horrified by the darkness and cold, he becomes aware of something moving fitfully in the sea. It is a round thing with trailing tentacles, hopping fitfully about in the blood-red water. Feeling faint and dreading the thought of being marooned in the silence and darkness, he is overcome with nausea. He seats himself on the machine and commences his journey back to his own time.

Chapter 12 was originally two separate chapters entitled "The Time Traveller's Return" and "After the Story." In conflating them Wells blurred the fact that two narrators are at work here. The first half of the chapter is narrated by the Time Traveler and describes his return to his home and friends in nineteenth-century Richmond. The second half, narrated by Hillyer, marks a resumption of the device contained in chapters 1 and 2—the descriptive *frame* enclosing the story.

The Traveler's narrative begins with an account of his journey through time to the familiar world he had left behind. The land ebbs and flows until, slackening speed, he recognises the architecture of his own age and sees the walls of his laboratory. Very gently he slows the machine down and comes to rest. As he does so he has the odd sensation of seeing in reverse the moment when he had begun his journey a week previously.

Having stopped the machine, he trembles violently but eventually calms down, glad to be back in his familiar surroundings. He tells himself that he might have imagined the whole experience, that the whole of his sojourn in 802,701 could have been a vivid dream. Then he grasps the fact that he had commenced his journey with the machine in the south-east corner of the laboratory but that it has come to rest in the *opposite* corner—this must be the precise distance between the little lawn where he had initially arrived and the White Sphinx.

Disheveled and hungry, the Traveler leaves the laboratory and moves toward the dining room. Before entering he notices a copy of the *Pall Mall Gazette* on a table and observes the date. Hearing the sounds of conversation and the clatter of plates he joins his friends at the meal.

He concludes his narrative by reminding them, "You know the rest. I washed, and dined, and now I am telling you the story." At this point Hillyer resumes his role as narrator. He describes the skepticism of the Editor and the Medical Man and the awkward pause that follows the Traveler's long story. "Taking it as a story," asks the Traveler, "what do you think of it?" Noting the doubt in the minds of his guests, he looks pointedly at the withered flowers and at the scars on his hands. The Medical Man says he does not recognise the flowers at all and asks if he can keep them; the Traveler refuses.

The Traveler himself then begins to have doubts and asks aloud whether the whole story was a dream. To settle his own uncertainty he returns to the laboratory to examine the Time Machine. The machine is there, apparently solid to the touch—Hillyer touches the rail of it—but soiled and with one rail bent askew. The guests then depart, and the Traveler bids them goodnight. The Editor tells Hillyer that he is convinced the whole story is a lie. Hillyer himself is undecided; the story has been incredible, yet it was so circumstantial and plausible in the telling.

The next morning Hillyer returns to the Traveler's house and asks to see his friend. On entering the laboratory he finds it empty; he pauses to have a closer look at the machine. He touches the lever and is astonished to see the whole mechanism sway "like a bough shaken by the wind." He finds the Traveler in another room carrying a camera and a knapsack. The Traveler explains that he is extremely busy with his machine and that he only needs half an hour to prove his story. He promises to return with specimens and proof. Hillyer then hears him enter the laboratory and close the door. Suddenly remembering that he has another engagement shortly, the narrator follows his friend but is too late—the Traveler has already embarked on another journey through time. The Time Machine has disappeared, and the laboratory is empty, apart from a subsiding swirl of dust.

Hillyer decides to wait, in the hope that the Traveler will return shortly with specimens and photographs. But he confides to the reader that "I am beginning to fear that I must wait a lifetime." The Traveler fails to return, and Hillyer is afraid he will never see his friend again.

The Time Machine ends with a brief epilogue in which the narrator speculates as to the Traveler's fate. Has he journeyed into the past and died at the hands of dinosaurs? Or did he go forward into another age, not the world of the Eloi and Morlocks but a nearer age, "in which men are still men"? Hillyer explains that the two of them had often discussed the future of mankind and that the Traveler had expressed grave misgivings concerning material advancement at the expense of the human spirit. As far as Hillyer is concerned, the future is unknown territory, "lit at a few casual places by the memory of his story." He then adds an eloquent coda: "And I have by me, for my comfort, two strange white flowers—shrivelled now, and brown and flat and brittle—to witness that even when mind and strength had gone, gratitude and a mutual tenderness still lived on in the heart of man."

The ambivalence of the epilogue is characteristic of all Wells's fiction; indeed, very few of his novels end on a note of resolution. Neither the reader nor the narrator knows whether the Time Traveler has journeyed to the future or the past, or even whether he is still alive. We simply do not know: "One cannot choose but wonder." Wells deliberately ends his narrative in this way in order to leave the reader in a state of uncertainty. It was a convention of the Victorian novel that all loose ends be neatly tied up in the concluding pages. By implicitly rejecting this device he signals the fact that his first novel marks a departure from the established parameters. It represents a new beginning.

NOTES

1. Wells, *Experiment in Autobiography* (London: Gollancz, 1934), 516.
2. H. E. Bates, *The Modern Short Story* (London: Michael Joseph, 1976), 110.
3. Leo Marx, *The Machine in the Garden* (New York: Oxford University Press, 1964), 229.
4. Wells, *Experiment in Autobiography*, 518.

3

Texts

The Time Machine did not spring into existence as a fully formed novel in 1895. It went through a complicated process of gestation spread over a period of eight years, in which it passed through draft after draft before Wells was satisfied. The aim of this chapter is to trace the evolution of *The Time Machine* from its first version published in 1888 to the publication of the version we know today, in the process offering insights into Wells's methods of composition and his artistic concerns.

THE CHRONIC ARGONAUTS

The earliest version of *The Time Machine* that can be traced with any certainty is *The Chronic Argonauts,* published in installments in the *Science Schools Journal* in 1888. The *Science Schools Journal* was founded in 1886 as the journal of the Normal School of Science. Wells was one of the founders and had been its first editor. It is highly probable that he had sought unsuccessfully to place *The Chronic Argonauts* in a commercial publication before submitting it to his old student magazine. In the event, it was published in the *Journal*, over his own name, in April, May, and June 1888, without any introductory or explanatory matter.[1] Bernard Bergonzi describes it as "the most ambitious and important piece of writing surviving from his earliest years."[2] It is important to regard it not as a short story but as a fragment of a novel, because that is clearly what it is. The decidedly leisurely manner of its opening makes it clear that Wells originally intended a narrative of book length and only broke it off when he realized it was unsatisfactory and that he could not complete it in its present form.

The story is set in Wales, in the village of Llyddwdd, and it seems safe to assume that Wells derived the Welsh setting from the months he spent at Holt, near Wrexham, in the summer and autumn of 1887. The plot of *The Chronic Argonauts* may be summarized as follows.

A mysterious stranger arrives at a ruined house called the Manse, half a mile outside the village, on the first day of May 1887. The superstitious villagers learn that the stranger's name is Dr. Moses Nebogipfel. Their fear of the newcomer is brought to a head when a local hunchback drops dead in a fit. An angry mob marches on the Manse, convinced that Nebogipfel is a "warlock" or a "witch." The vicar, the Rev. Elijah Ulysses Cook, goes in advance to warn him. When the villagers burst into the Manse, Nebogipfel and Cook are standing on a strange machine, and a moment later the two men vanish.

The second installment is set in the Fens. The narrator is lying by the edge of a lake, in deep thought, when a strange contraption appears, carrying two men. A clergyman steps from the machine and explains that he is the Reverend Cook. He seems greatly relieved to find that he is in the nineteenth century. Cook remains seriously ill for ten days but on his recovery explains that he wishes to make a statement about events in Llyddwdd and also about a murder alleged to have taken place there in the year 1862. Cook makes his statement and shortly afterward dies.

The third installment consists of the clergyman's statement, or deposition. In it Cook describes his encounter with Nebogipfel. Nebogipfel explains that his contraption is "a Chronic Argo," a machine that can travel through time. Nebogipfel explains the principles of time traveling and invites Cook to join him in his explorations. At this point the two men hear the mob outside shouting "Burn the warlock! Burn the murderer!" Nebogipfel seizes Cook, and they seat themselves on the machine. As the mob bursts into the room the two men embark on their journey through time, with "A thunderous roar like the bursting forth of a great fountain of water."

The story ends with these words:

> How did it end? How came it that Cook wept with joy to return once more to this nineteenth century of ours? Why did not Nebogipfel remain with him? All that, and more also, has been written, and will or will never be read, according as Fate may have decreed to the Curious Reader.

The abrupt ending must have been tantalizing to its original readers. Indeed, the editor of the *Journal* added the comment: "We believe that we express the general sentiment of our readers when we remark that it is a little too provoking for the ingenious writer to work up our interest to the highest pitch, and then leave us in the dark as to the sequel, in the manner he has done."

Despite the fact that the story is obviously incomplete and is written in overelaborate, Carlylean prose—Wells later termed his early style "Babu English"[3]—it is of considerable interest as the earliest surviving version of *The Time Machine.*

In *The Chronic Argonauts* we find one of the earliest and most sustained indications of that preoccupation with the future that was so characteristic of Wells. The Time Traveler describes himself as "a man thinking the thoughts of a wiser age . . . and now I go to join my generation, to journey through the ages till my time has come." *The Chronic Argonauts* was the first of a long series of prophetic writings including *The Time Machine, A Story of the Days to Come, When the Sleeper Wakes,* "A Dream of Armageddon," *The Discovery of the Future, The Shape of Things to Come,* and many others. As Wells said of himself: "I am extravagantly obsessed by the thing that might be, and impatient with the present; I want to go ahead of Father Time with a scythe of my own."[4] This obsession with the future is implicit in the story. A concern with *time* in all its aspects was to become one of Wells's most fundamental preoccupations, and in many of his novels and stories he experiments with time and duration. It is unclear whether or not he had read Sterne's *Tristram Shandy* before writing *The Chronic Argonauts*—certainly he had read it before writing *The Time Machine*—but there is a Sterne-like awareness of time and mortality about much of Wells's early writing.[5] The Time Traveler's describing himself as "a man born out of my time," "a man thinking the thoughts of a wiser age," and a man whose "age was still to come" are characteristic Wellsian touches.

The Chronic Argonauts is also significant because the Time Traveler, Dr. Nebogipfel, is the earliest example in Wells's writings of the solitary romantic hero. He can be identified as the precursor of Moreau in *The Island of Doctor Moreau,* Griffin in *The Invisible Man,* and Cavor in *The First Men in the Moon,* and he follows in a distinguished literary tradition including Frankenstein in Mary Shelley's romance and Dr. Jekyll in Stevenson's *Dr. Jekyll and Mr Hyde.* Nebogipfel is the scientist as magician, rather than the scientist as dispassionate man of reason. He is, moreover, solitary and secretive. He represents science as a symbol of the unknown. He is the scientist experimenting with unknown forces, with the forces of darkness, with powers he may be unable to control. *The Chronic Argonauts* is a story filled with fear, superstition, strangeness, and horror—not at all the kind of story one would expect from a student of Huxley. One has a sense of standing on the brink of the unknown, of peering into a world of strange and esoteric elements.

Throughout his literary career Wells was an experimental novelist, continually trying out fresh departures in narrative technique, in style, and in point of view. *The Chronic Argonauts* is an interesting early example of this practice. Part One of the story has the title "The Story from an *Exoteric* Point of View," and the subtitle "Being the Account of Dr. Nebogipfel's sojourn in Llyddwdd." This opening section is for the most part a straightforward piece of storytelling, describing the Manse, the village, the arrival of the stranger, the weird noises and lights in the Manse caused by Nebogipfel's experiments, the arousal of fear and superstition in the village, and the arrival of the crowd at the Manse. Part Two is entitled "The *Esoteric* Story Based on the Clergyman's Depositions," and it contains an account of the same events but this time looking at them from Cook's point of view. This contrast between exoteric and esoteric, between outward and inner, gives an interesting shift in perspective. Nebogipfel, instead of being an object of fear—almost of awe—becomes instead a harmless, rather kindly philosopher. Once he has explained his motives and intentions to the clergyman he becomes a man to be pitied, a man who deserves sympathy and understanding. One is reminded of the moment in *The Island of Doctor Moreau* when Moreau explains the truth and then asks: "And now what do you think? Are you in fear of me still?"[6] So already, in this immature story there are shifts in narrative method and point of view that foreshadow the mature Wells. Later he was to employ the same division between "exoteric" and "esoteric" in his short story "The Plattner Story" (1896).

There is no *certainty* about this story. It is a story filled with ambivalence and doubt. "The voyage," says the Time Traveler, "will be full of undreamt of dangers." In common with *The Time Machine* there is no conclusive ending. The Time Traveler vanishes with his machine—whether into the future or the past we do not know. This element of doubt is characteristic of Wells. The reader is simply left guessing. The story is neither optimistic nor pessimistic but ambivalent.

What is the significance of *The Chronic Argonauts?* Its significance, first, is that it can be regarded as the work through which a tyro taught himself the art of writing a novel. Between 1889 and 1892 Wells rewrote the story twice under the same title (unfortunately, these versions do not survive) and then between 1894 and 1895 rewrote it again four times before he was satisfied. His biographer Geoffrey West wrote, "This struggle to embody satisfactorily the brilliantly original idea of time traveling might in itself be said almost to constitute his literary apprenticeship."[7]

It says much for Wells that he continued working on this story—revising, reshaping, and polishing—often in the most lonely and dispiriting circumstances: at Holt, at Uppark, while he was a full-time schoolteacher at Henley House School in Kilburn, and during his unhappy first marriage. Clearly he was reluctant to abandon the idea, and sensed that in the concept of time traveling he had hit upon something original and important. With hindsight we can only be thankful for his patience and determination. Many aspiring writers would have given up after such a long apprenticeship.

But its greatest significance to literary history is that within its pages the basic idea of *The Time Machine* is clearly foreshadowed. The idea of time as the fourth dimension that forms an important element in *The Time Machine* is presented here in a recognizably similar form.

The notion of traveling through time has become so commonplace in science fiction that it is difficult for a modern reader to grasp how original the idea must have seemed a century ago. Wells was, of course, familiar with William Morris's *News from Nowhere* and such short stories as Irving's *Rip Van Winkle* and Poe's *A Tale of the Ragged Mountains,* but these feature a central character who either falls asleep and wakes to find himself in a different age or *dreams* he is transported to another time. The idea of a *machine* to journey through time was novel and seminal.

Above all, we find in *The Chronic Argonauts* that fusion of the ordinary and the fantastic that was to become the hallmark of Wells's scientific romances. The preoccupation with human behavior that is so evident in the Welsh chapters—the idiosyncrasies of the villagers, the evangelical fervour of the Calvinistic Methodists, the behavior of the crowd at the "Pig and Whistle"—is in sharp contrast to the fantastic story of the Time Traveler and his strange machine.

As a young man with an English accent suddenly thrust into a superstitious North Wales community (as had been his own lot as a schoolteacher), Wells had personal experience of the resentment and suspicion with which strangers were then regarded in isolated communities. He well knew that a stranger, and especially one of an unusual appearance, would be treated warily; he knew also the speed with which rumor and fear circulate in a village. The rural characters with which he peoples his story—though no doubt exaggerated—are recognizable, believable individuals. Wells was to make effective use of a village setting in *The Invisible Man* (1897), which also begins with the mysterious arrival of a stranger in a rural community. In *The Time Machine* the incredible story of the Time Traveler is set against a solid, believable background of a comfortable room in Richmond. Already discernible in *The Chronic Argonauts*, then—albeit in an embryo form—are some of the ideas and techniques that characterize *The Time Machine* and make it such a remarkable first novel. In its use of language and imagery, its preoccupation with the future, its emphasis on the romantic hero, and contrast between outer and inner perspectives, it anticipates much of Wells's later fiction and foreshadows the direction much of his writing was to take. Though crude and immature by comparison with his later work, it is an interesting illustration of the way in which disbelief can be suspended by placing extraordinary events within a familiar setting—a device he was to use with great effectiveness in his romances and short stories.

For many years *The Chronic Argonauts* was an extremely rare piece of Wellsiana. In the preface to the 1931 edition of *The Time Machine,* Wells wrote, "Already the writer had made an earlier experiment in the pseudo-Teutonic, Nathaniel Hawthorne style, an experiment printed in the *Science Schools Journal* and now happily unattainable."[8] In fact the story did remain unattainable until 1961, when it was published as an appendix to *The Early H. G. Wells,* by Bernard Bergonzi. Wells would have been surprised, and probably annoyed, to find that people were still reading *The Chronic Argonauts* a century after it was written. As an aspiring writer of twenty-one he was surely right to discontinue the story rather than attempt a task beyond his powers at that time. But he was wrong to dismiss the tale as of no consequence. The early work of a novelist is always of interest to students, but *The Chronic Argonauts* is of special significance as the first working of a vein that was to reach its full flowering in *The Time Machine* eight years later.

Though he had failed to secure publication of *The Chronic Argonauts* in a commercial journal and had felt obliged to discontinue its serialization, Wells was reluctant to abandon the idea and clearly felt that in the notion of time traveling he had hit upon something exciting and important. He continued to work away on successive drafts of the story and in September 1891 wrote to Frank Harris, editor of the influential *Fortnightly Review,* seeking his advice on publication: "Some days ago I left a copy of *The Chronic Argonauts*, a story you had very kindly promised to read, at Henrietta Street. I need scarcely say that whatever advice you can give me, for its disposal, will confer a great favour upon me."[9]

Harris had published Wells's seminal essay "The Rediscovery of the Unique" in the *Fortnightly Review* in July 1891 but declined to publish *The Chronic Argonauts* or another essay Wells submitted, "The Universe Rigid." (The version Harris read at that time would not have been the text published in the *Science Schools Journal* but a later revision.)

The text of the revised versions of *The Chronic Argonauts* written between 1889 and 1892 do not survive, but Wells's biographer Geoffrey West discussed these versions with Wells's former student friend Arthur Morley Davies, who had read and discussed them at the time. West gives the following account in his biography *H. G. Wells: A Sketch for a Portrait*:

> In the first rewriting Dr. Nebogipfel and the Rev Elijah Ulysses Cook still appear, but the scene shifts to a village on the South Downs. They arrive in a future much less changed from our time than that portrayed in *The Time Machine*. The upper and lower worlds exist, but their inhabitants are not yet two distinct species. A scientific aristocracy still survives in a decadent form as a red-robed priesthood, and art and literature are cultivated in a very dilettante manner. The Chronic Argonauts stir up these weary idlers, and even make it fashionable to read books. The priests take their visitors to see a vast museum, but themselves grow bored and leave the pair to explore alone, warning them against the passages that lead "down." They go "down," and discover an underworld working to support the upper world. Eventually some compunction is aroused among the aristocracy, and some kindly disposed persons descend to sing and play to the workers. At this the underworld explodes into revolution, kills them, and rushes up in a mob to carry out a general massacre. In the ensuing panic the Argonauts make for their machine. Cook has become fascinated by a certain Lady Dis, and tries to take her with him, but in the excitement of the escape he discovers that all her beauty is artificial, and flings her off as he climbs into the machine. They travel back to our own time, but overshoot the mark and are nearly killed by a party of Palaeolithic men. At last they hit the nineteenth century, when Nebogipfel drops Cook and then vanishes with the machine.
>
> In the third version, of which fragments only were read to me, Nebogipfel and Cook are cut out. There is no such underworld as in the earlier version and *The Time Machine,* the future being one in which a ruling class governs by hypnotism, but the end of the story is somewhat similar to that given above. One of the

> priests determines to put an end to the hypnotism and calls to the people to awake. They awake and kill him, and march with his head on a pole to slay his fellows. In the panic the same revelation is made of the artificial means by which the ruling class has hidden the physical degeneration resulting from their idle life. This third version never pleased me, and I was glad when *The Time Machine* went back to something nearer the original idea.[10]

It should be noted that the social order described in these two versions resembles that depicted in *When the Sleeper Wakes* (1899) rather than that described in any published version of *The Time Machine*.

THE *NATIONAL OBSERVER* TIME MACHINE

Early in 1894 Wells was invited by W. E. Henley, then editor of the *National Observer,* to contribute to that journal. William Ernest Henley was an influential critic and poet who had held a succession of editorial posts, including *London* and the *Magazine of Art,* and was a friend of R. L. Stevenson. Wells was flattered to receive an invitation from such a distinguished figure and decided to return to the idea of *The Chronic Argonauts*—an idea in which he had never lost faith.

Though Henley honored his promise to publish Wells's contributions, they were published at irregular intervals, with no introduction and without any indication that they were installments of a serial written by a single author. Moreover, the papers were unsigned.[11] The fact that they appeared anonymously and intermittently must have been disappointing to a hopeful author. Nevertheless Wells could console himself with the reflection that his work had appeared in the prestigious *National Observer* at Henley's own invitation. Clearly Henley had an eye for new talent, and Wells could only hope that the editor would remember him and continue to seek out his work in the future.

When the papers began to appear, Wells gave the impression that the articles were a revised version of *The Chronic Argonauts*. In March 1894 he wrote again to Davies, giving him an update on his literary work and adding, "I have also responded to an invitation of the *National Observer* and that old corpse of the Chronic Argo is being cut up into articles, one last Saturday (Time Travelling) one next number and possibly others to follow. It is quite recast. You might let me know what you think of it in its new garb."

In fact the *National Observer* articles bear little relation to the published version of *The Chronic Argonauts* but have many similarities with the book version of *The Time Machine,* though in fragmentary form. It is immediately apparent that the story has been fundamentally recast. In place of the melodramatic, rather overwritten tale set in a Welsh village there is a calm, philosophical narrative in which a lone traveler journeys to the future and seeks to learn all he can of the nature of civilization. The basic situation—that of a solitary explorer who finds himself in a strange country and tries to understand the ways of the people—clearly owes much to *Gulliver's Travels,* especially Part 4, "A Voyage to the Country of the Houyhnhnms." Wells acknowledged the influence of Swift on both *The Time Machine* and *The Island of Doctor Moreau,* and remained a lifelong admirer of his work.

All that the *National Observer* papers have in common with the earlier version would appear to be the discussion of time as the fourth dimension and the description of the time machine itself. Here is the description of the machine in the paper headed "A.D. 12,203":

> "What happened?" said the sceptical man, staring suspiciously at the squat framework of aluminium, brass and ebony, that stood in the laboratory. It was an incomprehensible interlacing of bars and tubes, oddly awry, heeling over into the black shadows of the corner as if to elude our scrutiny.

The descriptions of the machine in *The Chronic Argonauts,* the *National Observer* and final text have much in common, as may be seen from the following diagram:

Chronic Argonauts	*National Observer*	*Time Machine*
solid		solid
bars	bars	
	brass	brass
ebony	ebony	ebony
ivory		ivory
	squat	squat
awry	awry	awry

In all three cases one detects the sleight of hand through which Wells conveys a vivid impression of the machine without actually describing its appearance. The reader has a definite sense of a tangible invention without being told what it looked like.

Yet the differences between the *National Observer Time Machine* and *The Chronic Argonauts* are much more obvious than the similarities. There can be no question that the *National Observer* version is a considerable improvement on its predecessor and that, while the seven episodes suffer from being only loosely connected, this version marks a tangible advance, stylistically and imaginatively.

In form this version belongs to the genre known as "the tale within a tale." The narrator is not the Traveler himself but one of a group of friends who have assembled in the Traveler's comfortable home. Wells could, of course, have chosen to tell the story in the first person narrated by the Inventor but wisely decided to place the story within a frame. The reassuring setting and its "luxurious after-dinner atmosphere, when thought runs gracefully free of the trammels of precision" lull the reader into a comforting sense of the familiar in which it is easier to suspend disbelief. But the significance of the device goes beyond this. By placing the Time Traveler in a setting in which he is confronted by friends who are for the most part skeptical and matter of fact, Wells ensures that the Traveler is continually obliged to clarify and restate his propositions. He has to explain the principles of time traveling and describe his experiences in the future within a question-and-answer framework. Wells deeply admired the conversational novels of W. H. Mallock, especially *The New Republic* (1877), in which a group of friends assemble at a country house to discuss philosophy and culture. *The New Republic* was one of the most widely discussed works of its day, and Wells found its Platonic debate attractive. Years later he paid his own tribute to Mallock in *Boon* (1915), a conversational novel in which a number of friends discuss literature and ideas. The form of *The Time Machine* owes much to this device. This is particularly evident in the *National Observer* version, for at each stage of the narrative the Traveler is interrupted by one or other of his guests, who raise objections or introduce additional arguments. It is as if the Traveler is being cross-examined by a skeptical audience, each of his friends—the man with red hair, the very young man, the provincial mayor, the medical man, the commonsense person—raising doubts or introducing fresh perspectives. The reader has the sense that the story and its rationale have been viewed from a number of different angles and that every objection that could conceivably be raised to the tale has been considered. The reader becomes a member of the audience, sharing in their initial skepticism but suspending doubt as the story proceeds. The result is a marked advance in credibility. By means of this device the narrative is sifted through a critical process in which the Traveler, listening to and countering the arguments of his friends, convinces them that he has not only constructed a machine but has actually journeyed through time.

THE NEW REVIEW TIME MACHINE

Throughout 1894 Wells was living hand to mouth as a journalist, writing humorous articles and topical essays published for the most part in the *Pall Mall Gazette*. He and his wife-to-be, Amy Catherine Robbins, were living in lodgings on Mornington Road (now Terrace), Camden Town, but as both were in poor health and the summer heat of London was becoming oppressive they decided to spend the month of August in lodgings at Sevenoaks in Kent. The move was not a success. They were accompanied by Mrs. Robbins, who strongly disapproved of her daughter's liaison with Wells and lost no opportunity of telling them so. She was herself unwell and inclined to moods in which she would shut herself in her room. Both Wells and Amy were worried by his impending divorce from his wife Isabel. Moreover, his journalistic career, which had begun so promisingly, began to flounder. The *National Observer* was sold over Henley's head; the new editor disliked the time-traveling papers and truncated them abruptly. The literary editor of the *Pall Mall Gazette,* hitherto his staple source of income, went away on holiday, and his temporary assistant declined to accept Wells's contributions. The *Pall Mall Budget,* a weekly offshoot of the *Gazette* that had published a number of his short stories, announced it would shortly close. On top of all these worries, their landlady at Sevenoaks discovered their unmarried state and made life unpleasant for them with petty humiliations.

Despite these distractions a considerable amount of literary work was done during those weeks in lodgings, for Wells had an ambitious project up his sleeve. Henley had told him that he was starting a new monthly journal, *The New Review,* to be launched in January 1895, and that he wanted "The Time Traveler" as a serial. If Wells could rewrite the story as a continuous narrative instead of loosely connected instalments Henley would pay him a hundred pounds for the serial rights. Moreover, William Heinemann would undertake to publish the story in book form and would pay an advance of fifty pounds on a printing of ten thousand copies. To a young writer at the beginning of his career this seemed untold wealth (one would have to multiply these figures by at least thirty to arrive at present-day values), and he set to work to rewrite *The Time Machine* from beginning to end. Tusculum Villa, 23 Eardley Road, Sevenoaks, has some claim to a place in literary history as the house in which *The Time Machine* was born.

Wells's problem was how to transform the *National Observer* articles into a continuous story in which the Time Traveler would not merely have brief, tantalizing glimpses of the future but convey a detailed account of his adventures and a description of the future of civilization. In this task he was greatly encouraged by Henley, who was convinced that Wells possessed the ability to exploit the idea of time travel far beyond the glimpses contained in the *National Observer* papers. Wells set to work with feverish energy, beginning with paste-ups of the *National Observer* articles and proceeding through handwritten drafts and revisions of typed versions. He frequently worked far into the night on the warm summer evenings (much to the landlady's disgust, who considered he was using an excessive amount of lamp oil), and when not writing he and Amy would go for long walks amid the handsome beech woods of Knole Park. He wrote as one inspired, and when he came to write his autobiography forty years later still recalled the experience vividly:

> I sat alone at the round table downstairs writing steadily in the luminous circle cast by a shaded paraffin lamp. Jane [Amy Catherine Robbins] had gone to bed and her mother had been ill in bed all day. It was a very warm blue August night and the window was wide open. The best part of my mind fled through the story in a state of concentration before the Morlocks.[12]

By the end of the month he had completed a first draft of the complete story (not the final version of *The Time Machine* but a recognizable precursor of it) and submitted this to Henley for his comments. Henley wrote back enthusiastically, declaring "it is so full of invention, and the invention is so wonderful, so moving even—as I have found—that it must certainly make you a reputation."[13] Between September and December 1894 correspondence continued to flow between them as Wells submitted chapters and revisions for comment, Henley insisting "one reason why it was not a success elsewhere was that it was not a picture but a sketch." The story went through a succession of drafts before Wells was satisfied; it was published in installments in the *New Review* from January to May 1895.[14]

This version represents a considerable expansion of the *National Observer* articles, and while the previous version contained the basic idea and the skeleton of the story, the *New Review* version brought *The Time Machine* into a shape very much nearer its final form. In its literary and imaginative qualities, its mythological imagery, and narrative power, it is one of Wells's finest achievements. At the same time it embodies themes that remained characteristic of his work throughout his artistic career.

Stylistically, the *New Review* text, which Wells termed "The Time Traveler's Story," marks a distinct advance on its predecessor. While retaining the basic framework of the *National Observer* papers, Wells improved it dramatically by adding literary and descriptive touches, transforming the rather dry, impersonal tone of the *National Observer* version into an enthralling narrative. At the same time, a number of extraneous features present in the earlier version are silently removed (for example, one of the listeners is a German officer who speaks in the style of a stage villain—Wells wisely concluded that he added nothing to the plot and could be dispensed with). The result is a marked gain in fluency and clarity, combined with a great enhancement of literary power.

A striking feature of the *New Review* version that is not present in the book version published by Heinemann (the text with which most readers will be familiar) is the insistence in the opening paper that the universe is rigid and unalterable and that "if you grasped the whole of the present, knew all its tendencies and laws, you would see clearly all the future." In 1891 Wells had submitted to Frank Harris an essay containing this idea, "The Universe Rigid," which Harris had rejected as incomprehensible. Wells was chagrined by Harris's rejection but clearly felt the idea was an important one, for he returned to it again in his autobiography.[15] It is reasonable to assume that he incorporated some of "The Universe Rigid" material in the opening paper, though excised it from the book version—presumably because he felt it was too technical. The Time Traveler insists to his audience that "ordinary human perception is a hallucination" and that "the human consciousness is an immaterial something falling through this Rigid Universe of four dimensions, from the direction we call 'past' to the direction we call 'future.'" This conception of space and time remained with Wells throughout his life.

In the *National Observer* version of the story the Traveler journeys to the year 12,203. In the manuscript drafts Wells worked on at Sevenoaks the date is changed to 32,701, whereas in the *New Review* and the final version the date becomes 802,701. Wells evidently felt that ten thousand years hence was insufficiently far into the future for humanity to have divided into two distinct species, an objection that could also be raised to thirty thousand years hence (though curiously, due to an oversight, both the *New Review* and the first American edition refer to "the people of the year Thirty-two thousand odd"). Too much significance should not be read into the final choice of the date, beyond the fact that it is a falling sequence of numbers, as becomes clear when it is expressed in this form: 802 701.

Clearly Wells wished to suggest a world on the wane, a world running down toward its final extinction.

THE FIRST AMERICAN EDITION

The first book edition of *The Time Machine* was published by Henry Holt, in New York, on 7 May 1895. Since the first English edition was not published by Heinemann until three weeks later, on 29 May, the Holt text can claim to be the true first edition. However, it is the Heinemann edition that is now accepted as the final version.

The title page of the Holt edition includes an epigraph by Browning:

> Fool! All that is at all
> Lasts ever past recall.

The lines are taken from the poem "Rabbi Ben Ezra" and seem to suggest that the past is unalterable. Had Wells included the following two lines—"He (the creator) fixed thee 'mid this dance Of plastic circumstance, This Present, thou, forsooth, wouldst fain arrest"—there would be a hint that while the past cannot be changed, the present and future *can* be affected by human initiative.

Opposite the title page appears an "Author's Note" that is similar but not identical to that in the Heinemann edition:

> "The Time Traveler's Story" and a part of the introductory conversation appeared as a serial in the *New Review*. Several descriptive passages in the story had previously appeared in dialogue form in the *National Observer*, and the explanation of the "principles" of Time Traveling given in this book is inserted from the latter paper. I desire to make the usual acknowledgements.

The text of the Holt edition is a curious hybrid between the *National Observer* and *New Review* versions, suggesting that it marks a transitional text between the latter and the final version. It is difficult to determine the precise order in which the various drafts were composed, as there are no papers in the Wells Archive at the University of Illinois bearing on the Holt edition, and the records of Henry Holt and Company for this period do not survive. The matter is complicated by the fact that while parts of the text certainly predate the *New Review* version, other passages incorporate large parts of it. What can be said with certainty is that the Heinemann text is a more polished and more carefully revised version than the Holt text. It therefore seems fair to regard the latter as an early and intermediate version between "The Time Traveler's Story" as published by Henley and the first English edition.

In place of the eloquent epilogue that concludes the Heinemann version the Holt edition ends in this manner:

> Up to the present he has not returned, and when he does return he will find his home in the hands of strangers and his little gathering of auditors broken up for ever. Filby has exchanged poetry for playwriting, and is a rich man—as literary men go—and extremely unpopular. The Medical Man is dead, the Journalist is in India, and the Psychologist has succumbed to paralysis. Some of the other men I used to meet there have dropped completely out of existence as if they, too, had travelled off upon some similar anachronism. And so, ending in a kind of dead wall, the story of the Time Machine must remain for the present at least.

By comparison this is a strangely flat and unsatisfactory conclusion. Instead of the note of wonder with which the familiar text concludes, there is the rather pedestrian "Up to the present he has not returned." Particularly unsatisfactory is the final sentence: "And so, ending in a kind of dead wall, the story of the Time Machine must remain for the present at least." It is true that the words "for the present at least" hold out the possibility that the Traveler may one day return, but the phrase "ending in a kind of dead wall" has a finality that seems to preclude this. The style of the paragraph recalls the matter-of-fact beginning of the *New Review* version and altogether lacks the expressive and persuasive qualities of the final version.

Apart from the stylistic differences between the two versions, there are numerous differences of spelling, capitalization, and paragraphing that were presumably outside Wells's control; the Holt edition includes American spelling throughout and also contains far more paragraph divisions than Heinemann. Altogether one has the impression of an intermediate text that was outside Wells's jurisdiction once it had left his hands. Bernard Bergonzi concludes that "Wells may have virtually disowned the New York edition, since it represented an unrevised text, and this may account for his subsequent silence about it."[16] As it is it remains a literary curiosity, an intermediate stage between "The Time Traveler's Story" and the Heinemann version that is now known throughout the world.

THE FIRST ENGLISH EDITION

Between the autumn of 1894 and May 1895, when *The Time Machine* was published in book form, correspondence continued to flow between Henley and Wells. Henley clearly felt that the theme of traveling through time could be extended beyond the *New Review* episodes and urged Wells to elaborate the idea further. As late as 1 April 1895 Henley wrote to him in these terms:

> Of course, it would be tommy-rot to write in for the sake of lengthening out: but I confess that, as it seems to me, at this point—with all time before you—you might very well give your fancy play, and at the same time, oblige your editor. The Traveller's stoppings might, for instance, begin some periods earlier than they do, and he might even tell us about the last man and his female and the ultimate degeneracy of which they are the proof and sign. Or—but you are a better hand at it than I! I will add that I honestly believe that to amplify in some such sense will be to magnify the effect of the story.

There is some evidence from the surviving manuscripts that Wells toyed with the suggestion of traveling *backward* in time as well as *forward;* there is, for example, an episode in which the Traveler journeys to the year 1645 and is shot at with a musket. The writing is contrived and unconvincing, and he wisely omitted this passage from the published versions. That Wells felt uneasy with Henley's suggestions is clear from his introduction to the 1924 edition of *The Time Machine,* where he comments: "There was a slight struggle between the writer and W. E. Henley who wanted, he said, to put a little 'writing' into the tale. But the writer was in reaction from that sort of thing, the Henley interpolations were cut out again, and he had his own way with his text."[17] These "interpolations" apparently include the encounter with the kangaroo creatures and giant centipedes that forms part of "The Further Vision" in the *New Review* text but is excised from the Heinemann version.[18]

The principal difference between the *New Review* version and the first English edition of *The Time Machine* is in its opening scene. For the book version Wells, against Henley's advice, restored the introductory scene he had previously used in the *National Observer Time Machine*. Henley had felt it unwise to reproduce directly from the *National Observer,* but Wells thought quite properly that the original opening could not be improved upon. This substitution has a fundamental bearing on the evolutionary implications of the story. The *National Observer Time Machine* seemed to suggest that nothing is determined, that man is responsible for his own future, and that there is therefore a place for human will. The *New Review* introduction suggests the opposite—that the future is determined and unalterable. By placing so much emphasis on predestination Wells seemed to imply there can be no place for individual responsibility. In restoring the original introduction he removed the emphasis on determinism and left the way open for human choice. The Heinemann edition thus fuses together in a single artistic unity the best elements in the previous serial versions. From the *National Observer* he took the philosophical rationale of time travel, placed within its "frame" of a luxurious after-dinner atmosphere. From the *New Review* he took the narrative itself with its graphic vision of the Traveler's exploits in the world of 802,701 and culminating in the unforgettable "Further Vision," with its haunting picture of a dying planet and the blood-red sea. By fusing the two in a continuous narrative he removed the apparent ambiguity of the "Time Traveler's Story" and remained true to his own artistic concerns.

To summarize, then. The evolution of *The Time Machine* can be traced through a succession of stages:

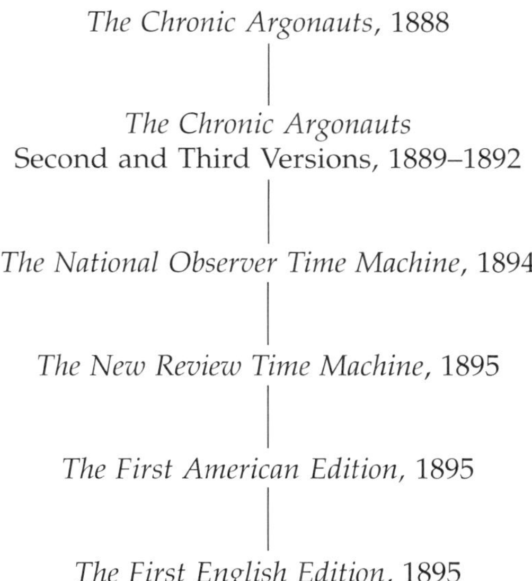

Even then Wells had not finished with his revisions. He was a compulsive reviser of his own work and continued to "tinker" with the text at intervals over the next forty years. Minor textual alterations were made in the Atlantic Edition of 1924, the Random House edition of 1931, and the collected edition of his works, *The Scientific Romances of H. G. Wells,* in 1933. But these textual emendations are minor (despite the drastic renumbering of the chapters for the Atlantic Edition). The essential text we know today, and the one with which students will be familiar, remains the Heinemann edition of 1895. It is this text that Wells launched on its long journey through time more than a century ago and that seems destined to earn for him literary immortality.

NOTES

1. The episodes were published as follows:
   Part I: no. 11 (April 1888), 312–20
   Part II: no. 12 (May 1888), 336–41
   Part III: no. 13 (June 1888), 367–71.

The Chronic Argonauts is included as an appendix in Bernard Bergonzi, *The Early H. G. Wells* (Manchester: Manchester University Press, 1961) and also in Harry Geduld, *The Definitive Time Machine* (Bloomington: Indiana University Press, 1987).

2. Bergonzi, *The Early H. G. Wells,* 25.
3. Wells, *Experiment in Autobiography* (London: Gollancz, 1934), 307.
4. *The Book of Catherine Wells* (London: Chatto and Windus, 1928), introduction, 27.
5. "A cleansing course of Swift and Sterne intervened before the idea was written again for Henley's *National Observer* in 1894." Preface to volume 1 of *The Atlantic Edition* (London: Fisher Unwin, 1924), xxi.
6. *The Island of Doctor Moreau*, chapter 14, "Doctor Moreau Explains."
7. Geoffrey West, *H. G. Wells: A Sketch for a Portrait* (London: Howe, 1930), 289.
8. Preface to *The Time Machine* (New York: Random House, 1931), ix.
9. Wells to Frank Harris, 5 September 1891.
10. West, *H. G. Wells: A Sketch for a Portrait,* 291–92.
11. The episodes were published as follows:
    1. 17 March 1894, 446–47
    2. 24 March 1894, 472–73
    3. 31 March 1894, 499–500
    4. 21 April 1894, 581–82
    5. 28 April 1894, 606–608
    6. 19 May 1894, 14–15
    7. 23 June 1894, 145–46.

The full text of the *National Observer Time Machine* is included in Robert Philmus and David Y. Hughes, eds., *H. G. Wells: Early Writings in Science and Science Fiction* (Berkeley: University of California Press, 1975) and also in Geduld, *The Definitive Time Machine.*

12. Wells, *Experiment in Autobiography*, 518
13. Henley to Wells, 28 September 1894.
14. The episodes were published as follows:

1, 2, and 3	January 1895, 98–112
4, 5, and 6	February 1895, 207–21

7 and 8	March 1895, 329–43
9, 10, 11, and 12	April 1895, 453–72
13, 14, and 15	May 1895, 577–88.

15. *Experiment in Autobiography*, 214–15, 222–24, 356–58

16. Bernard Bergonzi, "The Publication of The Time Machine 1894–5," *Review of English Studies* (February 1960): 42–51.

17. Wells, preface to volume 1 of the Atlantic Edition.

18. The text of this episode is included in E. F. Bleiler, ed., *Three Prophetic Novels of H. G. Wells* (New York: Dover, 1960), 325–27, and also in John Lawton, ed., *The Time Machine* (London: Everyman, 1995), 85–87.

4

Contexts

Wells arrived on the literary scene at a time of deep questioning in human affairs. New developments in science, invention, and philosophy challenged received attitudes and beliefs and widened the frontiers of thought. The year 1894, when he made his debut as a short-story writer, saw the discovery of argon, the construction of the first railway over the Andes, the first liquefaction of oxygen, and the publication of Benjamin Kidd's influential study *Social Revolution*. The following year saw the discovery of X-rays and the invention of wireless telegraphy and the cinematograph. These developments were paralleled by innovations in literature and the arts. The publication of *The Time Machine* in 1895 coincided with the emergence of Conrad and Stephen Crane, the rise of "modernist" music by Mahler and Richard Strauss, and the publication of Yeats's *Poems*. *The Time Machine* was written and published against a background of unprecedented change. The time was ripe for the emergence of a new author offering a strikingly fresh vision of the future.

THE LITERARY BACKGROUND

The close of the nineteenth century was a time of innovation in the English novel. The giants of Victorian fiction—Dickens, Thackeray, Trollope, George Eliot—were all dead, and a new generation of younger writers had taken their place. These included Conrad, Gissing, Kipling, and Wells, all of whom began publishing during the last two decades of the century.

The decade of the 1890s was an extraordinarily favorable climate for new writers. The 1870 Education Act had made schooling available to millions, and as a direct result there was now a rising generation of newly literate readers eager for lively, popular articles and stories. The great age of the "three-decker" novel that had dominated so much of the nineteenth century was drawing to its close, and in its place new writers were producing novels and stories more closely attuned to the needs of the time. The decade saw the publication of many fine collections of short stories, including Kipling's *Many Inventions,* Stevenson's *Island Nights Entertainments,* Gissing's *Human Odds and Ends,* and Conrad's *Tales of Unrest*. New journals were being launched to cater for the thousands of emerging readers, and their editors were eagerly on the lookout for writers of promise. George Newnes's *Tit-Bits* was founded in 1881, Alfred Harmsworth's *Answers* in 1888, and Arthur Pearson's *Pearsons Weekly* in 1890. By 1893 the circulation of *Tit-Bits* had risen to six hundred thousand copies a week, an indication of the enormous potential readership for popular journalism. In addition to the *Pall Mall Gazette,* which Wells described in a letter to his parents as "my bread and cheese," several London daily newspapers, including *St. James's Gazette* and the *Globe,* published short stories. To these must be added the established weeklies *Graphic, Black and White,* and the *Saturday Review,* all of which were in the market for stories. Wells was fortunate in beginning his literary career at the precise moment when originality and imaginative flair were most in demand.

The popularity of rail travel had produced a demand for short novels that could be read at a sitting. The pattern had been set by Stevenson's *The Strange Case of Dr. Jekyll and Mr. Hyde* (1886), which was swiftly followed by Conan Doyle's *A Study in Scarlet* (1887), Oscar Wilde's *The Picture of Dorian Gray* (1891), and Rudyard Kipling's *The Jungle Book* (1894). Novels of this kind were readily on sale at railway station bookstalls, and such organizations as W. H. Smith were quick to exploit the market. *The Time Machine* therefore appeared at a fortuitous moment in literary history. It was just at the point when the era of the classic Victorian novel had come to an end and a new phase was beginning. Readers and publishers were eager for fiction approaching the issues of the day with originality and insight.

THE SOCIAL BACKGROUND

The social climate was one of political and intellectual ferment. John Stuart Mills's *The Subjection of Women* was published in 1869, Darwin's *The Descent of Man* in 1871, and Henry George's *Progress and Poverty* in 1879. The debate on evolution generated by the teachings of Darwin and Huxley was raging all through Wells's early life. This ferment of ideas convinced him that he was living in an epoch of change and that the rigid, preordained world of his mother's generation was visibly passing away.

It was a time when education was being made available to a wider market, when new ideas of social reform were being disseminated, and many of the shibboleths of convention and privilege were being challenged. The first women students were admitted to Cambridge University in 1871, the Regent Street Polytechnic was opened in 1882, and the London School of Economics was founded in 1895.

It was also a time of new developments in the field of politics and anthropology. The Fabian Society was founded in 1884 (the same year in which Wells commenced his studies at South Kensington), a year that also saw the publication of Herbert Spencer's *Man versus the State* and the anarchist writings of Kropotkin. *Fabian Essays,* edited by George Bernard Shaw, appeared in 1889 and the Independent Labour Party in 1893. These developments coincided with the beginnings of psychoanalysis, the publication of William James's *The Principles of Psychology* and of Frazer's *The Golden Bough*. A spirit of enquiry was afoot—a movement of ideas in which the leading tenets that had dominated political and religious thought for much of the Victorian era were opened to debate.

The century had been dominated by a series of ideas that had permeated nineteenth-century thought: the idea of Progress, the idea of Empire, and the idea of Duty. Now these notions were increasingly being questioned.

THE END OF AN AGE

As the nineteenth century drew to its close there was widespread speculation concerning the new century and a sense that the Victorian era was coming to an end. The phrase *fin de siècle* (literally, "end of the century") was in circulation, signifying decadence and decline.

The literature of the fin de siècle was saturated with the idea of decadence, a mood that permeated all the arts throughout the 1890s. Urban decay and racial decline were dominant themes of "decadent" writers, particularly in evidence in the work of Arthur Machen and M. P. Shiel. The Eloi, with their languid lifestyle and suggestion of decline, are in some senses characteristic of the period: "They spent all their time in playing gently, in bathing in the river, in making love in a half-playful fashion, in eating fruit and sleeping" (42). Hedonism is one of the hallmarks of the decadent movement, exemplified by the main journal of 1890s aestheticism, *The Yellow Book*, which was closely associated with the work of Aubrey Beardsley and Oscar Wilde.

The darker side to the work of decadent writers was their preoccupation with the unexplored regions of the human mind and a fascination with diabolism and paganism. In this sense *Dr. Jekyll and Mr. Hyde,* with its depiction of a rational man torn by insensate desires, is characteristic of its time. Wells himself wrote a short story on a similar theme, "The Stolen Body" (published in 1898), describing a man who is possessed by an evil spirit and runs amok, committing acts of violence. The Morlocks, with their aura of bestiality and depravity, echo this fascination with the darker reaches of the mind. When the Traveler descends into their underground domain, he sees a world that he describes with words like "grotesque," "spectral," "oppressive," "obscene," "unmeaning." In drawing a contrast between the languorous eroticism of the Eloi and the sinister, malign Morlocks, Wells is dramatizing two of the dominant concerns of the period: aestheticism and decline, on the one hand, and the animal nature of man, on the other.

The Time Machine is a characteristic fin de siècle work in its emphasis on the future. As the nineteenth century drew to its close there was a widely shared awareness that the sun was setting on an age, and a growing curiosity as to what the new century would be like. But whereas many works of the period looked ahead to a golden age of happiness, Wells's emphasis is on decline and decay. The inhabitants of the upper world are described as "indescribably frail," "consumptive," "fragile." Their buildings are "profoundly time-worn," "collapsed," "rusting," "abandoned." The text is saturated with such words as *decline, sunset, twilight, waning, night.* Indeed, the most striking feature of *The Time Machine* is its pessimism. Instead of sketching a vision of the future in which man has perfected a prosperous, advanced civilization, the Traveler describes a world of ruined buildings and effete inhabitants living in fear of apelike Morlocks. The Traveler comments:

> I grieved to think how brief the dream of the human intellect had been. It had committed suicide. It had set itself steadfastly towards comfort and ease, a balanced society with security and permanency as its watchword, it had attained its hopes—to come to this at last. Once, life and property must have reached almost absolute safety. The rich had been assured of his wealth and comfort, the toiler assured of his life and work. No doubt in that perfect world there had been no unemployed problem, no social question left unsolved. And a great quiet had followed (78).

The Time Machine repeatedly stresses that material advancement may not necessarily lead to human happiness and that an increase in security leads to inertia and decline. The Traveler implicitly questions the assumption of the age that progress will continue unimpeded, suggesting instead that the growth of civilization will lead to a decline of the human spirit. His central thesis is that in a world where there is no struggle for existence, no new discoveries to be made, and no need for creative effort, man's surplus energies will find an outlet in eroticism and vice. In such a world there would be no need for thought, for books, for stimulus. It would be an age of "languor and decay." The novel suggests that man is living in an edifice of inertia and that henceforward he will decline, not rise.

This depressing prognosis presents a perspective of the future diametrically opposed to the mood of the time. Indeed, it is difficult for us today, living in a world of nuclear weapons, to imagine the impact the novel must have made a century ago. In 1894 the prevailing mood was one of optimism. Lord Rosebery was prime minister, presiding over a government concerned with issues of empire and trade. Oscar Wilde's *A Woman of No Importance* and Pinero's *The Second Mrs. Tanqueray* were the popular plays of the moment. In literature, Anthony Hope's *The Prisoner of Zenda* and Hall Caine's *The Manxman* were the current "best sellers." It was an age of confidence, opulence, and hope for the future. There seemed no reason why material progress should not continue unimpeded and indefinitely as the British looked forward to Queen Victoria's Diamond Jubilee in 1897.

Wells's vision flew in the face of this hopeful mood. William Morris's *News from Nowhere* and Edward Bellamy's *Looking Backward* had both given a rosy picture of a future in which all social problems had been solved. *The Time Machine* was in sharp contrast to such facile dreams.

TIME AND DISTANCE

To the reader in the twenty-first century, the description of the Time Traveler launching himself on his journey sounds quaintly old fashioned: "I gave it a last tap, tried all the screws again, put one more drop of oil on the quartz rod, and sat myself in the saddle" (18). One has to remember that *The Time Machine* was published when the cycling boom of the 1890s was at its height and when the motor car had recently been invented. Both these developments form part of the background to the novel.

The popularity of cycling had been greatly enhanced by Dunlop's invention of the pneumatic tyre in 1888. The bicycle made it possible for men and women to travel long distances with a freedom not previously enjoyed. Wells himself was a keen cyclist, and his novel *The Wheels of Chance* (1896) is filled with a sense of exhilaration, adventure, and exploration. Later he recorded in his autobiography that "the bicycle was the swiftest thing upon the roads in those days, there were as yet no automobiles and the cyclist had a lordliness, a sense of masterful adventure, that has gone from him altogether now."[1] The cycling vogue had an impact on women's dress, for it was cumbersome to wear a skirt while riding a bicycle; accordingly, emancipated young women took to wearing "rationals," trousers tucked into stockings below the knee. Rationals were considered greatly daring by the standards of the time and were frowned on by many of the older generation. When the Traveler notes that "in costume, and in all the differences of texture and bearing that now mark off the sexes from each other, these people of the future were alike" (29), Wells may have had in mind to some extent the impact of cycling on the fashions of the day. More importantly, the cycling boom contributed to female emancipation, for it dispensed with the chaperone hitherto considered indispensable for meetings between the sexes, and greatly enlarged the possibilities of travel, by freeing it from dependence on horse-drawn transport.

The invention of the internal combustion engine by Daimler and Benz in 1885 is even more pertinent to the genesis of *The Time Machine*. The early motor cars had many of the features of the horse-drawn cart and the bicycle: the first models had a saddle, a handle to steer with, and spoked wheels. Indeed, the primitive machines of the 1880s bear a striking resemblance to some artists' impressions of the Time Machine.

When the Traveler tells his sceptical audience that his machine is designed to travel "in any direction of Space and Time, as the driver determines" (7), he is speaking against a background of invention including the motor car, the first underground railway, and the first electric railway. What all these innovations—the bicycle, the internal combustion engine, the underground railway, and the electric train—had in common is that each of them enhanced freedom of movement by making it feasible to travel considerable distances at a fast speed. There is no mistaking the Traveler's sense of exhilaration when he embarks on his journey: "I drew a breath, set my teeth, gripped the starting lever with both hands, and went off with a thud" (18). Wells wanted the reader to share this joyous trepidation as his hero embarks on his journey into the unknown. At the same time he wanted his readers to be aware of the immense enlargement of human freedom made possible by new mechanical inventions. Later in his life he was fond of using the phrase "the conquest of distance" to symbolize the revolution in transport made by the railway and the aeroplane. *The Time Machine* is a product of its age in many senses, not least that it was written and published when mankind was on the brink of a far-reaching revolution in transport. This in turn had immense implications for attitudes toward distance and time.

MOTION PICTURES

The publication of *The Time Machine* also coincided with the invention of the cinematograph. The Lumière brothers, Auguste and Louis, are credited with having invented the cinematograph the very same year, 1895, but their invention had been anticipated by E. J. Marey as early as 1888 with his *chambre chronophotographique,* and again by Thomas Edison with his Kinetoscope, demonstrated in New York in 1894.

There is a direct link between *The Time Machine* and the coming of motion pictures, indeed, Wells's biographer Geoffrey West stated that Wells was "probably the first author of note to be brought into contact with the then embryo motion picture business."[2] A certain Robert W. Paul, a pioneer of the cinema, achieved in 1895 the first successful projection upon a screen. He read *The Time Machine* and was immediately struck by the possibility of simulating the experience of time travel through the device of a motion picture. He discussed this possibility with Wells, who met with him at Paul's office in London in the fall of 1895. The result was a successful application for a British patent that anticipated many of the standard techniques of the film industry including close-ups, fade-ins, and "dissolves" of scenes into one another. In the end, however, nothing came of the proposal. Wells did not pursue the matter, and Paul lacked the financial backing to take the idea farther.

The impact of the cinematograph upon *The Time Machine* remains an intriguing speculation. It seems clear that Wells's meetings with Paul did not take place until *after* the manuscript had reached its final form. On the other hand the *pictorial* quality of the narrative is so striking as to render irresistible the suggestion that Wells may have had in mind the possibility of depicting the narrative in a moving, visual form. What can be said with certainty is that *The Time Machine* is one of the most extraordinarily *visual* texts in literary history. In common with *Dr. Jekyll and Mr. Hyde* it is filled with graphic images that are fixed indelibly on the mind. This is one reason why the novel has exercised, and continues to exercise, a fascination for filmmakers.

It is also worth pointing out that the description of the Time Traveler returning from the distant future, slowing down, and then retracing in reverse the commencement of his journey vividly recalls the image of a film gradually winding down. That the writing and publication of the novel coincided with the invention of motion pictures underlines the fact that *The Time Machine* is one of those graphic texts that haunts literary history.

HAVES AND HAVE-NOTS

The end of the century was a time when manual workers were exploited, often toiling in difficult and dangerous conditions underground. As the Time Traveler expresses it: "So, in the end, above ground you must have the Haves, pursuing pleasure and comfort, and beauty, and below ground the Have-nots, the Workers getting continually adapted to the conditions of their labour" (50). One of the most striking aspects of Wells's vision of the future is his depiction of humanity divided into two separate species, the Eloi and the Morlocks. Where does this vision come from?

During the years when his mother was housekeeper at Uppark (1880–93) Wells was very definitely a "downstairs person." Large parts of the great house were completely out of bounds to him; both here and at his own home at Bromley he spent a considerable part of his life below stairs, not seeing natural light for hours on end. Uppark made a deep impression on him as a boy and a young man, not least because of its rigid hierarchical structure of staff and servants, and the sharp contrast between life above and below stairs. Wells's son Anthony West wrote many years later that *The Time Machine* could be regarded as "a violent gut reaction" to the world of Uppark.[3] The Time Traveler's attitude to the Morlocks is one of fear. They are described as "pallid creatures," "nauseatingly unhuman," "a new species of animal." In describing their troglodyte way of life and observing that the people of the upper world ignored their existence, Wells was extrapolating from trends already present in the world he knew. He had been born and brought up in a rigidly stratified world in which every human being "knew his place" and in which those above stairs regarded below stairs persons with fear and disdain. As he expressed it in his novel *Tono-Bungay* (1909). "In that English countryside of my boyhood every human being had a 'place.' It belonged to you from your birth like the colour of your eyes, it was inextricably your destiny. Above you were your betters, below you were your inferiors."[4]

The underground world of the Morlocks is not present at all in *The Chronic Argonauts*—though it appeared in the second (unpublished) version—but forms a central part of Wells's conception in all the published versions of *The Time Machine*. Given the stratified nature of Victorian England and the above-stairs/below-stairs world in which he spent his early life, it is not difficult to see why the division and contrast between an above-ground and a below-ground civilization formed such a central part of his picture.

It is the *rigidity* of society in Victorian England that the reader in the twenty-first century finds so difficult to comprehend. Living as we do in an increasingly mobile, fluid, and pluralistic civilization in which movement from one social class to another is commonplace, it is difficult to grasp the concept of a world where one's station in life was determined by one's birth. Wells himself, though the son of a gardener and a lady's maid, succeeded by his own efforts in escaping from his destiny and transforming the circumstances of his life. But he was of course highly exceptional; the prospects of the vast majority of those born in mid-Victorian times were circumscribed by their origins and parentage.

It was this ossified society that Wells sought to parody in his satirical vision of England in the year 802,701. It is interesting to note that before embarking on his journey into the future, the Time Traveler constructs a miniature version of the time machine, a model that is in every respect a copy of the full-sized version. In the same way Uppark can be seen as a microcosm for the Eloi and the Morlocks—what Wells has done is to extrapolate from the country house and estate he knew so well as a child to a picture of the whole world divided into above and below stairs. But already he senses that Uppark and all it represents is in decline. It is a world slowly crumbling, slowly but surely giving way to a new order of things.

PRECARIOUS MAN

The precariousness of man was a notion Wells had imbibed as a student of biology under Huxley. At South Kensington he had absorbed Huxley's dictum that nature was at worst hostile, at best indifferent—that, as Wells expressed it at the end of his life, "there is no reason whatever to believe that the order of nature has any greater bias in favor of man than it had in favor of the icthyosaur or the pterodactyl."[5] This stoical conception of the evolutionary process was one to which he adhered from his earliest student writings published in the *Science Schools Journal* in the 1880s to *Mind at the End of Its Tether* sixty years later. Many of the short stories witness to his belief in the unpredictable nature of man's environment. "In the Avu Observatory" describes an attack by an unidentified batlike creature; "The Flowering of the

Strange Orchid" depicts a blood-sucking plant; "The Purple Pileus" describes a poisonous fungus; "The Sea Raiders" is a gripping account of giant octopuses invading the English coast; "Aepyornis Island" postulates the hatching of a monstrous bird that attacks its human companion. Each of these stories implicitly challenges man's complacence by questioning the accepted notion of a benign universe.

In his autobiography he records of his early stories: "I was doing my best to write as other writers wrote, and it was long before I realised that my exceptional origins and training gave me an almost unavoidable freshness of approach and that I was being original in spite of my sedulous efforts to justify my discursive secondariness."[6]

One of the most interesting aspects of his freshness of approach was precisely his biological attitude to life—his conception that all living things were part of a single evolutionary process in a constant state of flux. The publication in 1871 of Darwin's *The Descent of Man* had been followed by a widespread misunderstanding and oversimplification of the theory of evolution, a misreading associated in the popular mind with a belief in the inevitability of progress and the essential goodwill of creation.

Wells's novel did not merely forecast an uncertain future for mankind but held out the prospect of a future in which man might not exist at all. In the closing chapters the Traveler postulates a cooling sun and a dying planet. The notion of man as one species among many, subject to the normal laws of evolution, must have jarred against the preconceptions of many contemporary readers, many of whom shared the widely held idea that evolution must inevitably lead to progress. There was a widespread misconception that the theory of natural selection postulated man as the culmination of a lengthy process of adaptation, and that *Homo sapiens* in his present form was—and must remain—the highest form of animal life. What was new and disturbing in Wells's thesis was its implicit rejection of this idea and its replacement by the recognition that ultimately man was doomed to extinction. In *The Time Machine* Wells compels his readers to face the unpalatable fact that progress is by no means inevitable, that man may be modified beyond recognition and ultimately may not even exist. This scenario, at once characteristic of Wells and disturbing in its implications, anticipates the pessimistic writings of his final years and reveals that even as a young man he was by no means the facile optimist of popular myth. The Time Traveler invites his audience to share his stoical acceptance of man's fate and in doing so implicitly rejects the complacence of the Victorian age.

Allied to this sense of the precariousness of the human condition is an awareness of the antiquity of man. One of the contexts surrounding the writing of *The Time Machine* was renewed attention to man's ancestry, stimulated by the discovery of the fossil remains of "Java Man" in 1890. The fossil evidence of *Pithecanthropus erectus* (literally "the ape man with an upright posture") was found in a stratum dating from the Upper Pleistocene era of 700,000 BC. The anthropologist L. S. B. Leakey states: "The discovery was an international sensation. No other fossil find had led to so many discussions or to so great a conflict of scientific opinion. The controversy raged for many years."[7] Wells must have been aware of the controversy surrounding the discovery, for at one bound man's ancestry had been located in the distant past. Instead of the idea that the earth and all its creatures had been suddenly created in 4004 BC (an idea insisted on by fundamentalists), here was evidence that the ancestors of *Homo sapiens* had been walking upright for immense periods of time. This awareness of the inconceivable distances of time—past and future—is continually in the background of the novel. It can be seen, for example, in the brooding image of the sphinx, with its suggestion of immemorial antiquity, and above all in the image of the derelict museum, with its insistent reminder of man's past achievements. One of the abiding impressions left in the mind after reading the novel is a consciousness of the human species as a product of time, both in the sense of past ancestry and that of future evolution.

THE END OF CERTAINTY

The debate over Darwin's theory of evolution was rumbling in the background all through Wells's adolescence. Coupled with this was an ongoing controversy concerning science and religion: Is there a benevolent order in the universe, a divine providence protecting us from evil, or must man shape his own destiny—without relying on a supernatural power?

Huxley had coined the word "agnostic" in 1869 to define his view that we have no certain knowledge of anything beyond material phenomena and that speculation regarding the supernatural is futile. Seeking to define the difference between his own views and those of orthodox believers, he wrote:

> The one thing in which most of these good people were agreed was the one thing in which I differed from them. They were quite sure they had attained a certain "gnosis"—had, more or less successfully, solved the problem of existence; while I was quite sure I had not, and had a pretty strong conviction that the problem was insoluble.[8]

The popular Victorian poet Matthew Arnold in his "Dover Beach" (1867) had used the image of the sea withdrawing from a beach to express his sense of a decline of faith:

The Sea of Faith
Was once, too, at the full, and round earth's shore
Lay like the folds of a bright girdle furl'd
But now I only hear
Its melancholy, long, withdrawing roar,
Retreating, to the breath
Of the night-wind, down the vast edges drear
And naked shingles of the world.

(It is interesting to note that both Arnold and Wells employ the image of a desolate beach—a striking metaphor).

Against this background the widely read novels of Charles Kingsley, R. M. Ballantyne, and others embodied the idea that the universe is ruled by a benign creator motivated by a concern for human welfare. This attitude to life, instilled into Wells from childhood by his devout mother, is implicitly rejected in *The Time Machine*. By putting forward a wholly secular account of the future of man, Wells must have antagonized many of his readers. In his vision there is no place for divine providence. The implication instead is that man's destiny lies in his own hands.

The Time Machine was a product of its age, in the sense that it embodies the fears and hopes of the end of the century. In its secular view, its stoicism, and its acknowledgement of the loneliness of the human condition it looks beyond the nineteenth century to the greater realism of our own time.

A PERIOD PIECE?

To what extent was *The Time Machine* characteristic of its time, and to what extent was it a new departure? In one sense it is very much a period piece: the Time Traveler wears "dingy nineteenth-century garments"; he wears a tail-coat; there is a reference to Lord Rosebery (prime minister from March 1894 to July 1895); a crab's antennae are likened to "carters' whips." The time machine itself has a *saddle,* inevitably suggesting a bicycle—a mode of transport then at the height of its popularity. In depicting the indolent Eloi and the brutish Morlocks, the book dramatizes phenomena much in the news in the 1890s—the languorous, decadent aesthetic movement of Oscar Wilde and Aubrey Beardsley, and the manual workers who spent much of their life underground or in darkness. In common with Samuel Butler's *Erewhon* and Edward Bellamy's *Looking Backward*, it looks at the future as a way of commenting on the present. On the other hand a novel that was simply a period piece would hardly have retained its popularity for a century after its publication. Clearly, *The Time Machine* possesses intrinsic qualities that have ensured its survival through changes in taste and literary fashion over a period of one hundred years. These qualities are, I believe, its enduring relevance as an allegory of the human condition and its haunting power as a vision of the future of man.

NOTES

1. Wells, *Experiment in Autobiography* (London: Gollancz, 1934), 543.
2. Geoffrey West, *H. G. Wells: A Sketch for a Portrait* (London: Howe, 1930), 294.
3. Anthony West, "My Father's Unpaid Debts of Love," *Observer*, 11 January 1976.
4. Wells, *Tono-Bungay* (London: Macmillan, 1909), book 1, chaps. 1, 3.
5. Wells, *The Fate of Homo Sapiens* (London: Secker and Warburg, 1939), 311.
6. Wells, *Experiment in Autobiography*, 509.
7. L. S. B. Leakey, *Unveiling Man's Origins* (London: Methuen, 1970), 62.
8. T. H. Huxley, "Agnosticism," in *Collected Essays*. Quoted in Leonard Huxley, ed., *Life and Letters of Thomas Henry Huxley* (London: Macmillan, 1900), 319–20.

H. G. Wells, circa 1876, aged ten. Photo courtesy of Bromley Libraries.

Uppark, West Sussex, where Wells's mother was housekeeper from 1880–93. *The Time Machine* can be read as a parody of the "upstairs/downstairs" world of Uppark. Photo courtesy of National Trust Photographic Library/Matthew Antrobus.

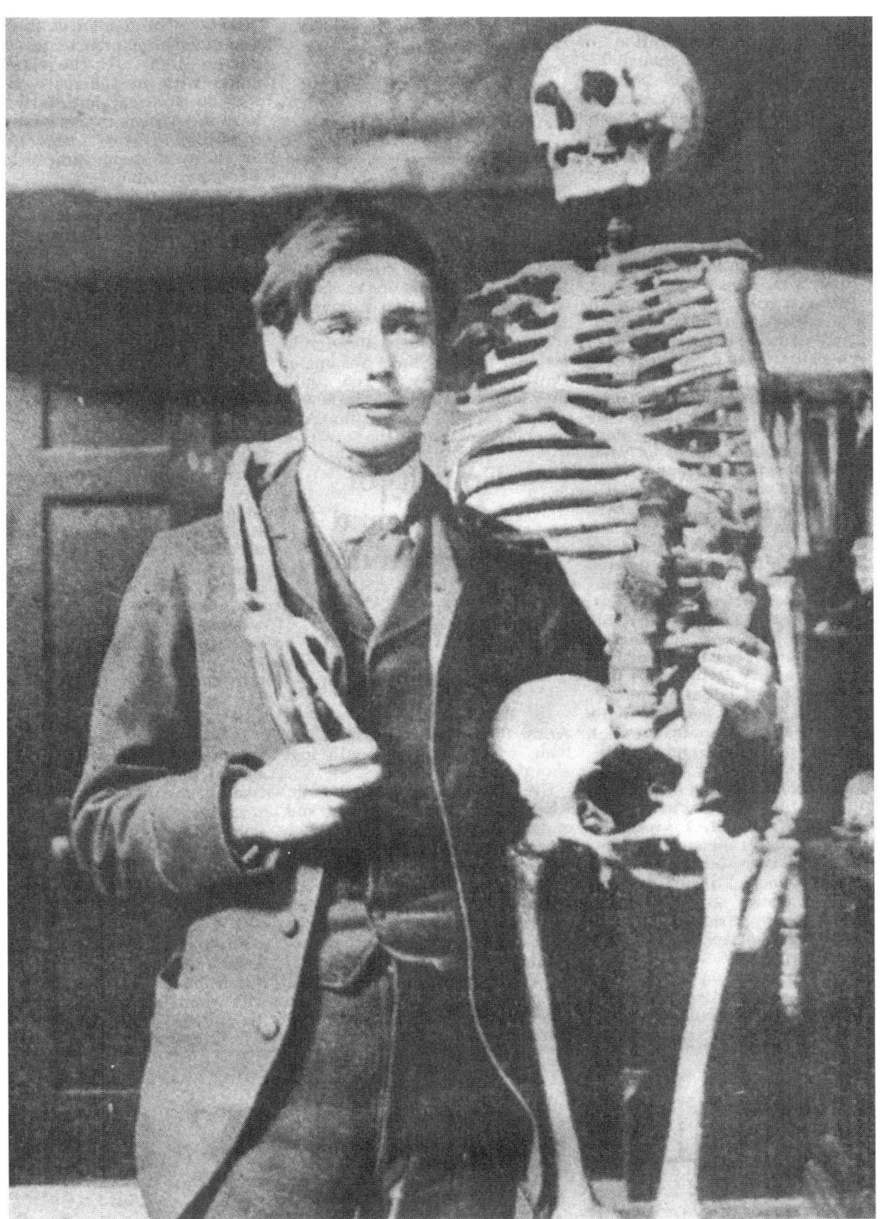

Wells as a science student at South Kensington, circa 1884. Photo courtesy of Imperial College Archives.

T. H. Huxley, whose biological vision of life deeply influenced Wells.

A page from the manuscript of *The Time Machine*, written at Sevenoaks, summer 1894. Courtesy of University of Illinois Library, Rare Book and Special Collections Library, Urbana-Champaign.

Tusculum Villa, 23 Eardley Road, Sevenoaks, Kent, the house where *The Time Machine* was written and revised.

H. G. Wells, circa 1900. Photograph taken by Jane Wells.

H. G. Wells at the height of his fame, 1930.

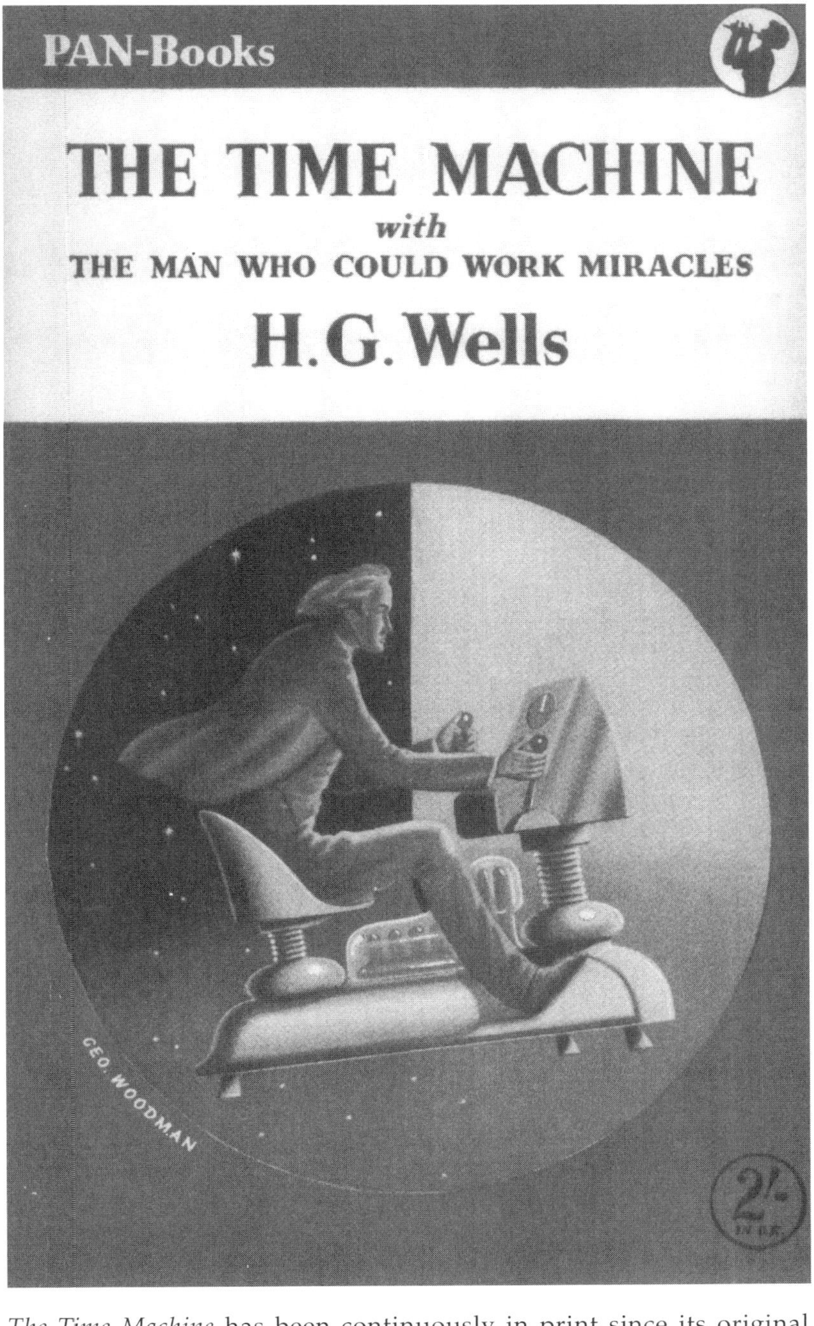

The Time Machine has been continuously in print since its original publication in 1895. Photo courtesy of Macmillan UK.

5

Ideas

> The typical plot of an allegory is one in which the "innocent"—Gulliver, Alice, the Lady in Milton's "Comus," K in Kafka's *The Castle*—is "put through" a series of experiences (tests, traps, fantasy gratifications) that add up to an imaginative analysis of contemporary "reality."
>
> —Roger Fowler, *A Dictionary of Modern Critical Terms*

> What have my books been from *The Time Machine* to *World Brain* but the clearest insistence on the insecurity of progress and the possibility of human degeneration and extinction? I think the odds are against man but that it is still worthwhile in spite of the odds.
>
> —H. G. Wells, letter to *British Weekly*, 26 June 1939

V. S. Pritchett has observed that *The Time Machine* "will take its place among the great stories of our language. Like all excellent works it has meanings within its meaning."[1] On what levels can the story be read?

The readings offered in this chapter are offered as possible readings only, without any sense of finality. *The Time Machine* is so rich in hermeneutic potential that it would be presumptuous to claim that any one interpretation can be definitive. The discussion that follows offers some *pointers* to possible ways in which the story can be read.

THE TIME MACHINE AS A QUEST

In common with many narratives depicting a journey—for example, Johnson's *Rasselas* and Conrad's *Heart of Darkness*—the Time Traveler's journey is both literal and metaphorical.

Literally, he travels far. The narrative is full of the vocabulary of a journey: "wandered," "proceeded," "pursued," "approached," "climbed," "walked." Reading the story one has a strong sense of a journey, not only in *time* but in *space*.

A word is necessary regarding the topography of the narrative. Despite the cosmic dimensions of his adventures, the Traveler never journeys far from the valley of the Thames. His journey begins and ends in his laboratory at Richmond, while the Palace of Green Porcelain is sited on hilly ground toward Banstead. During 1893 Wells had lived for a time at Sutton, and he knew the area around Sutton and Banstead well—see, for example, his essay "The Amateur Nature-Lover" (*Pall Mall Gazette,* 25 November 1893), a description of an autumn walk over Epsom Downs. While the story was in process of composition, Wells and Amy went for extensive walks from Sevenoaks over the Greensand Ridge, a wilderness of birch and pinewoods, bracken, heather, and gorse commanding views over the North Downs. It seems highly probable that these walks over hills and valleys suggested some of the terrain of the journey toward the Palace of Green Porcelain. The palace itself may have been suggested by Alexandra Palace, Muswell Hill, constructed in 1873. Alexandra Palace stands in a commanding position on the brow of a hill, and from it extensive views of the surrounding country can be seen; in Wells's time it stood in parkland covered with trees. Its façade is covered with decorative tiles resembling porcelain, and one can picture it bearing, in a ruinous condition, a striking resemblance to the building of his imagination. The Palace of Green Porcelain may equally well have been suggested by the Crystal Palace at Sydenham, which at one time contained stuffed animals and scientific exhibits such as those the Traveler describes.

So much for his literal journey. His metaphorical journey is a voyage into the unconscious. In one of the crucial episodes of the novel the hero is pursued through thickets by the Morlocks, and in the process his beloved Weena loses her life. The thickets are an obstacle preventing the hero from reaching his goal. His journey can be seen as a metaphor for life itself, for the valley of experience and travail through which all must pass. Those journeying across the valley are impeded by a series of obstacles—woods, thickets, darkness, the Morlocks—

symbolizing all those forces of resistance and inertia that hamper personal fulfilment.

There are numerous parallels between *The Time Machine* and the quest legends of the Holy Grail. In an illuminating study of Alain-Fournier's *Le Grand Meaulnes* (a novel that has some affinity with *The Time Machine*), Robert Gibson has highlighted the conventions of the fairy tale: the monsters the hero regularly encounters on his travels, the dark forest that frequently needs to be traversed, the fairy castle.[2] The classic fairy tale frequently employs the number three: three blind mice, three brothers, three wishes. The same pattern is repeated in *The Time Machine*—the fruit eaten by the Traveler has a three-sided husk, he wakes to find "three stooping white creatures," there are three fruit trees in the open court of the Palace of Green Porcelain, in the fight in the forest there are three Morlocks at his feet, and, finally, he vanishes "three years ago." This repetition of motifs based on a threefold pattern reinforces some of the novel's underlying themes. The figure three traditionally represents birth, life, and death (or creation, preservation, and extinction). The Traveler's arrival in 802,701 is comparable to a new birth—"I felt naked in a strange world"—while his adventures parallel the human journey toward enlightenment and final death.

The landscape of the story frequently resembles that of a fairy tale: the narrator writes of "the tall pinnacles of the Palace of Green Porcelain and the polished gleam of its walls"; he refers to lush valleys, sleeping houses, and "a little open court within the palace." As if to underline the analogy with *The Sleeping Beauty,* stress is laid upon Weena's unconsciousness: "She seemed scarcely to breathe. . . . I tried what I could to revive her, but she lay like one dead. I could not even satisfy myself whether or not she breathed" (73–74). Fairy tales are often symbolic dramatizations of the painful journey from adolescence to maturity. From this point of view *The Time Machine* is unusually interesting in both psychological and metaphorical terms.

One reason why the story has such a powerful hold on the imagination is that it contains strong mythological elements. The basic plot of a lone visitant struggling against the forces of darkness conforms to the classic theme of the quest, in Arthurian romance. The Palace of Green Porcelain that so intrigues the Traveler resembles, when seen from a distance, the enchanted castle in a medieval tale of chivalry. Weena, whom he rescues from drowning and seeks to protect from the Morlocks, corresponds to the rescued princess of legend. The thickets through which they struggle in their flight symbolize the forces of darkness and danger they must traverse if they are to be free. (Note the Arthurian echoes of the Traveler's use of the word "mace" to describe the metal lever he uses as a weapon, an allusion made even more explicit when the Traveler goes forth "mace in one hand and Weena in the other"). The perilous journey across an unknown landscape is common to many mythologies from time immemorial, as is the Traveler's passing through a series of trials and obstacles. In this sense the story can be seen as a modern version of an ancient story. The Traveler's descent into the well recalls the voyage to the abyss of the underworld in the legend of Psyche and Cupid, while his fight with the Morlocks is an echo of comparable struggles in many literatures.

In his quest to defeat the Morlocks and regain possession of the Time Machine, the Traveler becomes a representative figure. He becomes the knight of Arthurian legend, the romantic hero determined to outwit his adversaries and rescue the sleeping princess (Weena) from the forces of darkness and evil. Joseph Campbell in *The Hero with a Thousand Faces* has shown how many fables and legends from different ages and literatures are based on the idea of the journey: the quest through an enchanted landscape, pitted with unknown dangers, toward a castle or refuge: "Once having traversed the threshold, the hero moves in a dream landscape of curiously fluid, ambiguous forms, where he must survive a succession of trials. This is a favorite phase of the myth-adventure. It has produced a world literature of miraculous tests and ordeals."[3]

By imagining a protagonist who is transposed into an alien world and must then traverse a hostile landscape in search of an enchanted castle (the Palace of Green Porcelain), facing all manner of perils on the way, Wells dramatizes this central myth in an acute form.

THE TIME MACHINE AS AN ALLEGORY

That Wells intended an allegorical interpretation underlying the surface narrative is apparent from the extensive use of mythological and dream imagery. At the conclusion of his story the Traveler poses the question whether it is all a dream: "They say life is a dream, a precious poor dream at times" (88). Wells's deployment of conventional symbols for a *threshold*—the broken window caused by the departure of the machine from the laboratory, the clap of thunder that greets his arrival in 802,701, the doors beneath the sphinx that must be opened before he can regain his machine—represent the transition from conscious to unconscious, from the world of everyday reality to the world of the mind. *The Time Machine* is a voyage not only into the future but into the unconscious. By dramatizing fundamental aspirations and fears in the form of an allegorical fable, Wells created a myth of continuing relevance to our times.

The fact that the Traveler is not named adds to the symbolic quality of the story. In all the 1894–95 versions he has no name; he is simply referred to as the Philosophical Inventor, the Inventor, or the Time Traveler. Like Christian in *The Pilgrim's Progress* he is Everyman, a sample human being with the normal complement of anger, fear, hunger, and despair. Because he is fallible and subject to moods of disgust and self-doubt, the reader identifies with him in his plight, sharing in his adventures and his attempts to understand the world around him. It is this timeless element that gives the story the quality of a parable, a myth of universal relevance.

The story can be read as an allegory of the human condition, with its central situation of a solitary protagonist pitting his intelligence against forces of darkness and danger until finally reaching his goal. The myth of a lone survivor seeking to triumph over obstacles placed in his path by adversaries whose language and motivations he does not understand holds a seminal place in literature and forms the central theme of Samuel Butler's *Erewhon* and Swift's *Gulliver's Travels*. The Traveler has to solve the riddle of life for himself; the whole of his sojourn in the year 802,701 can be seen as an effort to solve the riddle posed by the inscrutable white figure of the sphinx. Not only does the sphinx lie at the center of the story in the sense that the Traveler cannot travel very far from it—"a certain feeling, you may understand, tethered me in a circle of a few miles around the point of my arrival" (40)—but it quite literally holds the key to his future, for, unknown to him, the Time Machine lies imprisoned within it. (Wells here echoes the Greek legend of a sphinx that waylaid travelers and tormented them with a riddle; if they could not answer, it devoured them.)

The languor and indifference of the Eloi are in the sharpest contrast to his own resolve to change his circumstances:

> It behoves me to be calm and patient, to learn the way of the people, to get a clear idea of the method of my loss, and the means of getting materials and tools; so that in the end, perhaps, I may make another [37].
>
> Face this world. Learn its ways, watch it, be careful of too hasty guesses at its meaning. In the end you will find clues to it all [39].
>
> Still, however helpless the little people in the presence of their mysterious Fear, I was differently constituted. I came out of this age of ours, this ripe prime of the human race, when Fear does not paralyse and mystery has lost its terrors. I at least would defend myself [58].

The Traveler refuses to submit to his fate but uses his intelligence, cunning, and resourcefulness to defeat his adversaries. His message to his listeners—who are for the most part complacent about or skeptical toward his story—is that man must pit his intelligence against unknown forces, must rely on his own ingenuity to combat complacence and evil. Man's destiny, in short, lies in his own hands. The point is made explicit when the Traveler descends into the underworld and, confronting the Morlocks, observes: "I stood there with only the weapons and the powers that Nature had endowed me with—hands, feet, and teeth" (55). In Wells's vision there is no inherent contradiction between predestination and free will; there is still a role for individual choice even in a universe that is an unalterable apparatus. On the one hand the story can be regarded as a deeply pessimistic fable; indeed, David Lodge has described it as "one of the most desolating myths in modern literature."[4] On the other hand it can be regarded as an *optimistic* fable, in the sense that the Traveler, by employing all his resources of intelligence and strength, succeeds in outwitting his enemies and triumphing over his environment. From this standpoint the story is a vindication of the human spirit.

The Traveler has no resources but his own ingenuity and his physical strength. With these resources he must pit himself against a hostile universe, including his formidable adversaries the Morlocks and a race of giant crabs. By his strength and skill he at last outwits his opponents and triumphs over his own demise. From this standpoint it is apparent that *The Time Machine* should be seen alongside other myths that illustrate the human condition in allegorical form, including such works as Swift's *Gulliver's Travels,* Johnson's *Rasselas,* Conrad's *Heart of Darkness,* and Bunyan's *Pilgrim's Progress*. The central situation of a protagonist overcoming a series of obstacles in quest of an elusive goal provides a rationale for the novel that amply justifies it in artistic terms and gives heroic stature to the Time Traveler. He is at once the solitary hero in quest of enlightenment and Man seeking against all odds to triumph over adversity.

In the eloquent epilogue the narrator, reflecting on the Traveler's adventures and speculating on his destiny, comments:

> He, I know—for the question had been discussed among us long before the Time Machine was made—thought but cheerlessly of the Advancement of Mankind, and saw in the growing pile of civilization only a foolish heaping that must inevitably fall back upon and destroy its makers in the end. If that is so, it remains for us to live as though it were not so [91].

Even when the odds against him seem insuperable, he must still live "as though it were not so," each individual doing his utmost within the limits of his powers to change his environment. Viewed in this light, the novel is a characteristic Wellsian text. In portraying man's predicament through the fable of the Time Traveler and emphasizing the crucial importance of human intelligence, Wells dramatizes the contrast between determinism and choice and places the central emphasis on individual responsibility.

DISSOLVING VIEWS

One of the principal underlying themes of the novel is *change*. Even before the Traveler arrives at his destination the reader has an impression of a landscape in a state of flux:

> The landscape was misty and vague. I was still on the hill-side upon which this house now stands, and the shoulder rose above me grey and dim. I saw trees growing and changing like puffs of vapour, now brown, now green: they grew, spread, shivered, and passed away. I saw huge buildings rise up faint and fair, and pass like dreams. The whole surface of the earth seemed changed—melting and flowing under my eyes [19].

The language here heightens the sense of a landscape in process of transformation—"growing," "changing," "melting," "flowing." Already the narrator is preparing the reader for the idea that the world of the future will be utterly different from the familiar world he has left behind.

On arriving in 802,701 his first impressions are of familiar sights: a lawn, a garden, rhododendron bushes, a silver birch tree. This is immediately followed by enigmatic sights: a sphinx, huge buildings, figures clad in robes. The contrast between the known and the unknown sharpens the notion of change; the Traveler has passed from a world of reassuring familiarity to one of strangeness. When, later, he begins an exploration of this new world, he is struck by its total unlikeness: "Here and there among the greenery were palace-like buildings, but the house and the cottage, which form such characteristic features of our own English landscape, had disappeared" (29). The contrast is even more marked by our awareness that although the Traveler has journeyed far in *time* he has hardly moved at all in *space*. The marble statue of the sphinx is physically only a short distance from his laboratory. At the end of the novel the desolate beach that forms such a haunting vision is in the same *location* as his home in Richmond. There is no description of an epic journey, as in Rider Haggard's *She* or Edgar Allan Poe's *The Narrative of Arthur Gordon Pym;* instead, we have an awareness of fundamental change literally on our own doorstep.

Wells's image of "the whole surface of the earth . . . melting and flowing under my eyes" is a powerful one that is implicit throughout the narrative. He is anxious that his readers share with him this sense of a world in process of continuous change. The young Wells, born at the height of the Victorian age in a hierarchical society that must have seemed immovable, deliberately puts forward the opposite concept—the idea of a society utterly different from the known world of everyday.

In his novel *Tono-Bungay* Wells uses the phrase "Dissolving Views" to convey his sense of society in a process of flux:

> The new order may have gone far toward shaping itself, but just as in that sort of lantern show that used to be known in the village as the "Dissolving Views," the scene that is going remains upon the mind, traceable and evident, and the newer picture is yet enigmatical long after the lines that are to replace those former ones have grown bright and strong, so that the new England of our children's children is still a riddle to me.[5]

The Time Machine was the first of a long series of visions of the future from Wells's pen—a genre he termed "fantasias of possibility." These included *When the Sleeper Wakes* (1899), *A Modern Utopia* (1905), *The World Set Free* (1914), and *Men Like Gods* (1923). What these have in common is that each is kinetic rather than static: each of his visions presents a picture of a society that is changing *and that can be changed* as a result of human initiative. It is this aspect of *The Time Machine* that makes it stand out as a product of its age.

DISENTANGLEMENT

The story has a more personal relevance to Wells in his lifelong attempts to disentangle himself from restricting circumstances. Psychologically, it can be seen as a dramatization of Wells's personal struggle to free himself from his past and from all the forces holding him back (the underground rooms at Bromley and Uppark, the claustrophobic world of the draper's shop, his humble origins) and triumph over adversity.

In the context of Wells's struggle to free himself from the forces impeding him, it is interesting to note the frequency with which images of being pulled back recur in *The Time Machine*: "She began to pull at me with her little hands" (53), "I disengaged myself from the clutches of the Morlocks" (56), "I felt as if I was in a monstrous spider's web" (74), "I was caught by the neck, by the hair, by the arms, and pulled down" (74), "The clinging hands slipped from me" (80). In his short story "The Apple" (1896), the narrator has to pass through "dry branches that stuck like thorns" and "grass like knife blades" before finding the Apple of the Tree of Knowledge, while in "Mr. Skelmersdale in Fairyland" (1901) thorns, briars, and twisted roots separate the narrator from the Anima figure of his dreams. Thickets, briars, and other impedimenta frequently recur in dreams and mythology.[6]

Seen in these terms, *The Time Machine* is unusually interesting both as a metaphor and from the point of view of Wells's own psychology. The Time Traveler outwits his adversaries and triumphs over his enemies, the Morlocks and the giant crabs. Wells, in writing the story, launches himself on his literary career and frees himself from all the forces of inertia and convention holding him back. From this perspective it is very much a young man's book; he was twenty-eight when he wrote it. Looking back on it later he commented, "It seems a very undergraduate performance to its now mature writer."[7] It has much in common with other novels of adolescence, including *Le Grand Meaulnes* and John Fowles's *The Magus*—the heuristic mill the protagonist has to undergo, the yearning for enlightenment, the enigmatic Anima figure. All three novels possess a childlike quality in which the central figure struggles to make sense of a world he does not understand.

Disentanglement forms a powerful theme in Wells's fiction. In such stories as "The Valley of Spiders," "The Flowering of the Strange Orchid," "The Sea Raiders," and "The Country of the Blind" there are striking images of entrapment. These are particularly vivid in *The Time Machine*, for there is a strong sense of being pulled irresistibly downward: "I was clutched by several hands," "They were trying to haul me back," "I was violently tugged backward" (56). The Traveler's escape from the clinging Morlocks and emergence to the surface is paralleled by Wells's escape from drapery and from his cramping environment (see, for example, his comment in his autobiography: "Retail trade, I thought, had captured me for good.")[8] In the light of his numerous attempts to escape from his destiny it is interesting to note the Traveler's description of the sensations of time traveling as "a kind of hysterical exhilaration" (19). One reason why *The Time Machine* is such a compelling narrative is that the reader shares with the storyteller a sense of *exhilaration* at his adventures.

The reader is aware that for all his human weaknesses, the Traveler has triumphed. The Morlocks have failed to capture him. They have also failed to construct a time machine of their own and therefore cannot pursue him. The reader is an observer looking at the Traveler from the outside but also identifies with him, sharing his sense of victory at having outwitted his pursuers.

Note also that in traveling far into the future the Traveler is disentangling himself from his own death, just as Wells, by writing a work that will outlast himself, has triumphed over his own demise. Wells's health as a young man was very poor, and there were times when he genuinely feared for his life. Writing to his old student friend Arthur Morley Davies in May 1888, he declared, "I have coughed up recently a lot more of gory lung, so I am afraid the hungry maw will presently engulf the Prophet of the Undelivered Spell, and the unwarned world hurry on to damnation." In writing *The Time Machine* he hoped to ensure that his name and reputation would continue beyond his physical death and thus score a victory over human mortality.

UTOPIA AND ANTI-UTOPIA

An ironic tone is evident in much of *The Time Machine*, suggesting that Wells had a satirical intention in mind. He is satirizing not only the dichotomy between the aristocracy and the dispossessed, and the aestheticism of Oscar Wilde and his circle, but an important genre of English literature—the utopian romance. By the close of the nineteenth century the conventions of the genre were well established. There is an apparently reliable narrator who describes a sojourn in an idyllic land, a fortuitous meeting with a guide who explains the basis of the social order and how it came about, a wholly consistent explanation of all that the narrator sees, a "happy" ending in which all doubts in the narrator's mind are satisfactorily resolved, and a conclusion expressing his desire to return to the arcadia of his dreams. Wells turns each of these conventions on its head.

In place of the calm narrative authority of such a utopia as Edward Bellamy's *Looking Backward* or W. H. Hudson's *A Crystal Age,* we are faced in *The Time Machine* with a narrator who is divided against himself—professing to be a man of science but prone to moods of anger, doubt, frustration, and despair. Nor is the reader wholly convinced that the Traveler is a reliable witness; Hillyer, the narrator of the opening chapter, tells us, "The fact is, the Time Traveller was one of those men who are too clever to be believed: you never felt that you saw all round him" (12). There is an element of doubt about some of the Traveler's explanations, Hillyer hinting at several points that he is not totally convinced by the veracity of the story. When the Traveler has finished his account of his adventures in the year 802,701, neither the Editor nor the Medical Man believes his tale. For a moment the Traveler himself has reservations about the reality of his experiences and has to be convinced by seeing and touching the machine. In contrast, such a narrator as Julian West in *Looking Backward* or Smith in *A Crystal Age* seem motivated wholly by reason, neither doubting the explanations given to them nor giving the reader cause for skepticism.

The device of the fortuitous encounter with an omniscient guide is altogether absent from Wells's vision—"I had no convenient cicerone in the pattern of the Utopian books" (50). In place of the trustworthy commentator such as Dr. Leete in *Looking Backward* or Hammond in *News from Nowhere,* the Traveler has to deduce what he can of the nature of society through a process of discovery and inference. He is fully aware of the dangers in this approach—"Conceive the tale of London which a negro, fresh from Central Africa, would take back to his tribe!" (41)—and at a number of points confesses to the reader that his deductions may be wholly wrong. Toward the end of his first day in 802,701 the Traveler offers an explanation for the apparent decline of civilization and then comments: "Very simple was my explanation, and plausible enough—as most wrong theories are!" (34). On his final day with the Eloi he theorizes for the last time on the divergence between the Eloi and the Morlocks, warning the reader that "it may be as wrong an explanation as mortal wit could invent" (79). In place of omniscience, then, there is ignorance and doubt. The Traveler freely confesses his explanations may be erroneous and that he may have glimpsed only a small facet of the truth. The reader of *The Time Machine* is not presented with a fully worked-out vision of a future society but instead with a fragmentary and subjective picture filtered through the observations of a single eyewitness. On his own admission the eyewitness is impulsive, impatient, and irrational. Instead of a coherent framework of society, fully elaborated in all its details, we have a blurred picture—vividly wrought and convincingly told but blurred and incomplete nevertheless.

In *The Time Machine* there is no neat ending with all loose ends resolved. Instead, the novel ends on an enigmatic note, leaving many questions in the mind of the reader. Has the Traveler journeyed into the future or the past? Is he still alive? What is preventing him from returning to his own time? Above all, there is a conspicuous absence of that longing to return to the future that is such a feature of the utopian romance. Instead, we find the opposite—the Traveler muses on "the years I had spent in study and toil to get into the future age, and now my passion of anxiety to get out of it" (39). There is no mistaking his eagerness to escape from the world he has found, nor his longing to return to his home: "I began to think of this house of mine, of this fireside, of some of you, and with such thoughts came a longing that was pain" (77).

The predominant tone of the novel is one of gentle mockery of the accepted norms of the romance. Wells is satirizing the utopian romance and in doing so cannot resist a note of ridicule of the pretensions of the genre. This can be seen in the Traveler's touch of humor at his own naiveté: "The memory of my confident anticipations of a profoundly grave and intellectual posterity came, with irresistible merriment, to my mind" (25); his sideswipe at *News from Nowhere,* "I had no convenient cicerone" (50); and his bitter humor at his own self-confidence, "I thought of my hasty conclusions upon that evening, and could not refrain from laughing bitterly at my confidence" (77). His self-doubt is in the sharpest contrast to the facile presumption of *Looking Backward*. Instead of a future in which social conflict has been resolved, Wells's vision is one of society in a state of unending tension.

The Time Machine is not a utopia on the pattern of those by Bellamy, Morris, and Hudson. It is rather an anti-utopia, or *dystopia*—a satire commenting on the present in the guise of a description of the future. During the past century the dystopia has become a commonplace of science fiction, but this does not detract from the measure of Wells's achievement. In highlighting the inherent defects of the utopian romance and challenging its assumptions he anticipates the work of later writers, including Orwell and Huxley.

THE TIME MACHINE AS HISTORY

"And during these few revolutions [of the stars] all the activity, all the traditions, the complex organizations, the nations, languages, literatures, aspirations, even the mere memory of Man as I knew him, had been swept out of existence" (61–62).

To a reader at the close of the Victorian age the notion of the extinction of man would have seemed unthinkable, even laughable. The idea that humanity might one day come to an end was totally alien to his way of thought. The mood of the time favored the opposite idea—that man would go on from strength to strength surmounting one achievement after another, with no conceivable limit to his enterprise. In his essay "The Extinction of Man," written while *The Time Machine* was being composed, Wells had pointed out that "in no case does the record of the fossils show a really dominant species succeeded by its own descendants" and had stressed that "in the case of every other predominant animal the world has ever seen[,] . . . the hour of its complete ascendancy has been the eve of its entire overthrow."[9] This insistence on the possibility of human extinction forms the theme of a number of his short stories, including "The Sea Raiders" and "The Empire of the Ants," while the notion of a malign universe finds expression in such fables as *The Island of Dr. Moreau* and *The War of the Worlds*. Wells's novel is an assault on human complacence and a reminder that *Homo sapiens* is not immutable. *The Time Machine* compels the reader to face the possibility that the human species is changing, that it may not always be supreme, and that in the future it may evolve in ways we cannot at present foresee.

The novel can be read as a *history*, presenting an overview of human evolution from the beginning to the end. Note that at the conclusion of the Traveler's story, in his haunting vision of the earth thirty million years hence, man has come full circle. He has returned to the sea from which he emerged as a species in primordial times: "It was a round thing, the size of a football perhaps . . . and tentacles trailed down from it; it seemed black against the weltering blood-red water, and it was hopping fitfully about" (85). Wells's vision is disturbing in its starkness. For the Victorian reader, and for the reader in the twenty-first century, there is no escaping the bleak realism of *The Time Machine*—the empire of man is finite.

As a history of the future the novel can be seen as the forerunner of a series of anticipations that flowed from Wells's pen, including *When the Sleeper Wakes* (1899), *The World Set Free* (1914), and *The Shape of Things to Come* (1933). But his first novel is breathtaking in its audacity and sweep. For in this short work he foretells the end of culture (books and reading are clearly a thing of the past), the end of the Christian religion, the end of world order, and the end of man himself. It is hardly surprising that he described the novel as "my trump card."[10] He well knew that *The Time Machine* was daring in its vision and that it marked a new departure in English literature.

AFTER *THE TIME MACHINE*

What happened next? *The Time Machine* ends on a note of uncertainty: "One cannot choose but wonder," as the epilogue expresses it. Wells never wrote a sequel to the novel, and there is no evidence that he would have authorized a sequel from another hand. Since his death in 1946 a number of sequels have been written, including *Morlock*

Night, by K. W. Jeter (1978); *The Man Who Loved Morlocks*, by David Lake (1981); and *The Time Ships*, by Stephen Baxter (1995). That so many authors have tried their hand at writing sequels is testimony to the vitality of the original story and to a continuing interest in the Traveler's adventures. Why did Wells himself never attempt to continue the story?

It can be argued that the ambivalent ending is central to Wells's design and that it is precisely *because* the reader is left in suspense that the story is so intriguing. A sequel with all loose ends tied up and all ambiguities removed would destroy the illusion so carefully created by the author. Central to his purpose is the wish to stimulate thought and provoke speculation concerning the future, not only the Time Traveler's personal future but in a wider sense the destiny of the Eloi and Morlocks. We must not lose sight of Wells's fundamental thesis—his insistence that man's destiny lies in his own hands and that the future *can* be shaped by human initiative.

He did not wish to write a sequel for the very good reason that the story is complete in itself. Despite the fact that it ends on a note of irresolution, it is as he intended it to be—a parable offering a vision of human evolution and deliberately ending in ambiguity. It is a short novel, but in it he said all he wanted to say within the limits of his design.

It is germane to this argument to ask the question: What was the author's own attitude to the novel? How did he regard his own handiwork? In the preface to *The Time Machine* in the collected edition of his works published in 1924 he wrote, "And now the writer reads this book, *The Time Machine*, and can no more touch it or change it than if it were the work of an entirely different person. He reads it again after a long interval, he does not believe he has opened its pages for twenty years, and finds it hard and 'clever' and youthful."[11]

Here we see the mature Wells—who was by then a world figure and the author of the best-selling *Outline of History* and numerous widely read novels—looking back on his youthful self. In a preface to the 1931 edition of the novel he again looked back on himself as an apprentice writer learning his craft, but this time with a note of affection: "One must err to grow and the writer feels no remorse for this youthful effort. Indeed he hugs his vanity very pleasantly at times when his dear old *Time Machine* crops up once more in essays and speeches, still a practical and convenient way of retrospect or prophecy."[12]

The truth seems to be that Wells regarded *The Time Machine* as the work of a young writer at the beginning of his literary career. He looked back on it with affection as his first novel, and as the work through which he taught himself the art of writing fiction.

When it was published in 1895 he could have had no inkling then that he had written a work destined to take its place alongside the classic texts of the past. What he *did* know was that his novel was well received, that it established his reputation, and that he had "arrived" on the literary scene. He was content.

WARNING OR PROPHECY?

Is the story a warning or a prophecy? At the conclusion of his narrative the Traveler raises either possibility when he declares: "Take it as a lie—or a prophecy. Say I dreamed it in the workshop. Consider I have been speculating upon the destinies of our race, until I have hatched this fiction" (87). Whether warning or prophecy, the implication is that the future pattern of civilization *can* be affected by human initiative, that man is not simply a passive observer (as the Traveler's audience are of his story) but an active participant. The human story is the Traveler's story writ large. One reading of the story, then, is a salutary one—that the future *can* be changed through man's own efforts, that Man is responsible for his own destiny. The implication is that the Traveler *can* alter his personal future by returning to the year 802,701 and rescuing Weena from the Morlocks.[13] In a wider sense man as a species *can* shape the future of the planet.

As a *warning* Wells's novel is surely one of the seminal texts of the nineteenth century. Coming as it did at a time of confidence in material progress and complacence regarding human destiny, the message of *The Time Machine* was wholly apposite. It is worth emphasizing the narrator's conclusion that even if civilization is doomed to collapse, "*it remains for us to live as though it were not so*" (91, my italics). Wells never forgot Huxley's injunction that "all question of the future apart, this life as it can be lived, pain, sorrow, and evil notwithstanding, is worth—and well worth—living."[14]

In his essay "What I Believe" (1899), Wells observed that each of his scientific romances pointed a moral and that *The Time Machine* was meant to suggest "the responsibility of men to mankind."[15] This is evident at many points in the narrative, most obviously in the implied plea for the application of humane values to social evolution. It can also be seen in the Traveler's determination to rescue Weena from drowning, in his concern for the welfare of the Eloi, his grief at their lack of concern for one another, and in the narrator's reassurance at the end of the novel that "gratitude and a mutual tenderness still lived on in the heart of man" (91). In its emphasis on the human values of sympathy and compassion and its regret at their loss, *The Time Machine* is a warning that material progress at the expense of the human spirit is futile and ultimately doomed to failure.

The Time Machine is a heroic book, a brave book. When Wells struggled with successive drafts at Tusculum Villa, Sevenoaks, during the hot summer of 1894 he can have had little conception that he was creating a work of art that would in the course of time achieve classic status. "Things written either live or die," he wrote later; "unless it be for a place of judgment upon academic imposters, there is no apologetic intermediate state."[16] In the course of its hundred-year history *The Time Machine* has never occupied an "apologetic intermediate state" but has been continuously in demand. It is available in a variety of editions, both popular and scholarly, and continues to be read for both study and enjoyment. This little book is imbued with the qualities that will ensure for Wells a lasting place in literary history—a sense of wonder, poetic imagination, and vivid narrative power. Above all, it epitomizes that ability to create a myth of enduring relevance to the human condition, a myth that may yet prove to be his finest contribution to life and thought.

NOTES

1. V. S. Pritchett, *The Living Novel* (London: Chatto and Windus, 1946), 120.
2. Robert Gibson, *Le Grand Meaulnes* (London: Grant and Cutler, 1986), 103–104.
3. Joseph Campbell, *The Hero with a Thousand Faces* (London: Paladin, 1988), 97.
4. David Lodge, *Language of Fiction* (London: Routledge and Kegan Paul, 1966), 223.
5. Wells, *Tono-Bungay* (London: Macmillan, 1909), book 1, chap. 1.
6. "The Apple" and "Mr Skelmersdale in Fairyland" are both included in John Hammond, ed., *The Complete Short Stories of H. G. Wells* (London: J. M. Dent, 1998).
7. Wells, preface to *The Time Machine* (New York, Random House, 1931), ix.
8. Wells, *Experiment in Autobiography* (London: Gollancz, 1934), 147.
9. Wells, "The Extinction of Man," *Pall Mall Gazette*, 25 September 1894. This essay is included in *Certain Personal Matters* (London: Lawrence and Bullen, 1898), 172–79.
10. Letter to Elizabeth Healey, 22 December 1894.
11. Wells, introduction to vol. 1 of *The Atlantic Edition of the Works of H. G. Wells* (London: Fisher Unwin, 1924), xxii.
12. Wells, Preface to *The Time Machine* (New York: Random House, 1931), x.
13. Note, however, the formidable theoretical obstacles preventing the Traveler from intervening in Weena's predicament. If he returned to 802,701

there would then be *two* Travelers; it is difficult to see how Wells could have surmounted this difficulty. Several sequels to *The Time Machine* attempt to solve this problem, most notably Stephen Baxter's *The Time Ships* (1995). Wells was certainly aware of it, for he discussed it in his essay *The Betterave Papers*, commenting "it is plain common sense that a man might multiply himself indefinitely, pop a little way into the future and then come back. There would then be two of him" (*Cornhill Magazine*, July 1945, 361).

14. Leonard Huxley, ed., *Life and Letters of Thomas Henry Huxley* (London: Macmillan, 1900), 403.

15. Wells, "What I Believe," *Puritan*, April 1899, i.

16. *The Country of the Blind and Other Stories* (London: Nelson, 1911), introduction, ix.

6

Narrative Art

> A study of the successive versions that he made of *The Time Machine* between the summer of 1894 and the spring of 1895 suggests that the young Wells had an artistic scrupulosity almost rivalling that of James himself.
>
> —Bernard Bergonzi, "The Publication of *The Time Machine*," *Review of English Studies* 11, no. 41 (February 1960): 51

In drawing attention to Wells's "artistic scrupulosity," Bergonzi highlights the most striking feature of *The Time Machine*: its literary craftsmanship. The fact that Wells lavished such pains on the novel as it passed through draft after draft suggests that he was fully aware of its literary and imaginative qualities. He would not have written it with such care had he not been convinced that the novel would make or break his literary reputation. He knew also that its central idea was of fundamental importance in both scientific and artistic terms and that it merited the utmost attention he could bring to it.

THE READER AND THE TEXT

While we are reading the novel there are three processes simultaneously at work: (a) The Traveler is telling his story, (b) the audience is listening to the Traveler, and (c) the reader is following the text. These processes flow seamlessly into one another.

The close relationship between reader and text is heightened by the fact that at a number of points in the narrative the Traveler addresses the reader directly:

> You who have never seen the like can scarcely imagine what delicate and wonderful flowers countless years of culture had created (25).
>
> Can you imagine what I felt as this conviction came home to me? (34).
>
> But I did not stay long to look, I promise you (56).
>
> You may imagine how all my calm vanished (80).

This device of addressing the reader as "you" enhances the sense of immediacy. It is as if Wells is talking to us directly—the reader becomes a participant in the storytelling process. The author arouses our interest and curiosity, inviting us to share the Traveler's predicament and seeking our emotional involvement. The reader is no longer a passive consumer of the text but an active participant in the narrative process, sharing vicariously in the Traveler's adventures as he experiences curiosity, fear, disappointment, anger, and grief.

When reading a novel told in the first person, it is tempting to assume that the "I" who is telling the story and the author are one and the same. Yet Wells was careful to distinguish between his first-person narrators and himself. In the case of *The Time Machine* the distinction is particularly interesting, because the Time Traveler is not so much Wells himself as Wells *as he aspired to be*.

At the time of writing the story, he was a young man in poor health earning a precarious living as a journalist. He had had little literary success and was just beginning to make a name for himself as a short-story writer. The Traveler, in contrast, is clearly a man of substance. He is a respected scientist and author, a published writer whose work has appeared in the *Philosophical Transactions*. He has a comfortable home in Richmond, complete with servants, elegantly furnished rooms, and a laboratory. It seems safe to assume that for the young Wells, earning his "bread and cheese" as a freelance journalist, the Traveler represented all that he aspired to in terms of success and prosperity.

TAKING IT AS A STORY

After the Traveler returns to his Richmond home and gives his account to his skeptical audience, he concludes: "Treat my assertion of its truth as a mere stroke of art to enhance its interest. And taking it as a story, what do you think of it?" (87).

Taking it as a story is an interesting phrase and is a reminder both of the Traveler's curiosity to know how his audience has reacted to his tale and of Wells's own eagerness to know the reader's response. We can reply with confidence that *taking it as a story,* the narrative is of compelling interest and offers convincing evidence of Wells's skill as a storyteller. The novel is not only of exceptional interest as a study in myth and imagery but also a fascinating case study in narrative technique. It is worth taking a closer look, for example, at the way in which the novel is *structured.*

The story reads so fluently that it is easy to overlook the fact that it is skilfully paced. All the time the Traveler is telling his story he is, of course, aware of the way in which the story ends, but this knowledge is not imparted to his listeners or his readers. Instead, he keeps his audience guessing until the very end. First he describes the sensations of time traveling, then his arrival in 802,701, then a detailed account of his reception by the Eloi and first impressions. This is followed by his speculations concerning the nature of the future society ("The Sunset of Mankind" is his original chapter heading). This is immediately succeeded by a graphic account of the missing time machine and his agonized response. A further chapter of speculation follows (headed "Explanation" in the Heinemann edition), then an account of his descent into the underground world of the Morlocks, his friendship with Weena, and their journey to the Palace of Green Porcelain. Then comes his pursuit by the Morlocks, the death of Weena, and his final escape from the trap of the White Sphinx.

All this is narrated in a measured way, incident by incident, carefully combining vivid description with abstract reasoning. The Traveler is *unwinding* his story, keeping his audience in suspense at every stage, sharing with them his inferences and discoveries but holding his cards close to his chest.

While following the narrative the reader has a sense that everything being described is happening *now.* There is an extraordinary sense of immediacy, as if we are watching a film unfolding before our eyes. This is greatly enhanced by the *pictorial quality* of Wells's imagination. The scene in which the Traveler first arrives in 802,701, for example, or his explorations in the Palace of Green Porcelain, are etched indelibly on the imagination. (If the reader compares these scenes with the central episodes in *When the Sleeper Wakes,* it will be seen at once that *The Time Machine* possesses literary qualities that the later romance does not to the same degree).

The pacing of the narrative is matched by the symmetrical structure of the novel as a whole. The novel opens with the *descriptive frame* we noted earlier (pages 3–17). The frame is followed by the Traveler's account of his adventures (pages 17–87), which is told without a break, apart from the brief moment when he places on the table the flowers put in his pockets by Weena. The novel is rounded off by a resumption of the framing device (pages 87–90), in which the Traveler answers questions put to him by his guests. The final pages are thus a mirror image of the opening. This balanced structure is a marked advance on the somewhat clumsy structure of Samuel Butler's *Erewhon* or Edward Bellamy's *Looking Backward,* in which the narrator's adventures simply peter out.

The phrase "mirror image" is literally true, for on his return to Richmond the Traveler sees his housekeeper walk across the laboratory and remarks that "now her every motion appeared to be the exact inversion of her previous ones" (86). There is a sense of unwinding a film, comparable to the moment in *Alice through the Looking Glass* when Alice steps through the mirror.

Note also that Hillyer, the "outer narrator," makes his own contribution to the suspense of the story. Immediately before the Traveler commences his narrative, Hillyer sets the scene by remarking: "You read, I will suppose, attentively enough; but you cannot see the speaker's white, sincere face in the bright circle of the little lamp, nor hear the intonation of his voice. You cannot know how his expression followed the turns of his story!" (17). This is more than a mere literary touch to enhance the verisimilitude of the story. By stressing his own fascination with the Traveler's narrative Hillyer greatly adds to the conviction of the novel—he is absorbed in the story himself and wishes to pass on his total immersion to the reader.

Also, it is Hillyer who adds the eloquent epilogue speculating on the fate that has befallen the Traveler. It is Hillyer who is comforted by the strange flowers, "not unlike very large white mallows," and it is he who puts on record the Time Traveler's story and thus preserves it for posterity.

A TRANSPARENT NARRATIVE

The first clue that the narrative is not as straightforward as it appears is contained in the novel's subtitle: "An Invention." This clearly refers to both the time machine itself as an artifact and the story as a fictional creation. At a number of points in the story, the reader's attention is drawn to an element of unreality in the appearances of things:

> "This little affair," said the Time Traveler, resting his elbows upon the table and pressing his hands together above the apparatus, "is only a model. It is my plan for a machine to travel through time. You will notice that it looks singularly askew, and that there is an odd twinkling appearance about this bar, as though it was in some way unreal" (9).
>
> I stared for a minute at the Time Machine and put out my hand and touched the lever. At that the squat substantial-looking mass swayed like a bough shaken by the wind (89).
>
> I seemed to see a ghostly, indistinct figure sitting in a whirling mass of black and brass for a moment—a figure so transparent that the bench behind with its sheets of drawings was absolutely distinct; but this phantasm vanished as I rubbed my eyes (90).

These references to an apparently solid world that was "in some way unreal," to a figure who is so transparent that he is referred to as a "phantasm," should alert the reader to the fact that it is not simply the time machine that is insubstantial but the narrative itself; one is invited continually to look both at it and through it.

In entering *The Time Machine* the reader is embarking on an imaginative quest in which nothing is as it seems. What appears to be a solid, reliable narrative proves, on examination, to be a labyrinth capable of many different interpretations.

At intervals throughout the story one becomes aware that the author is gently toying with the reader. There is a deliberate mocking of the interpretative process, as if the narrator is offering solutions to the riddle of the sphinx only to discard them one by one. The Time Traveler's own interpretations of the riddle are initially wholly erroneous. The first solution offered to the reader is a vision of humanity on the wane. The narrator elaborates a picture of a world "of perfect comfort and security," a society in which men live in utopian harmony in a state of ease and balance. Having developed this theory at length and convinced himself that he has "mastered the whole secret of these delicious people" the narrator warns the reader that it is false. "Very simple was my explanation, and plausible enough—as most wrong theories are!" In the following chapter he puts forward the theory that mankind has differentiated into two distinct species, the Eloi above ground and the Morlocks below ground, and that the two live in a state of equilibrium. Humanity has become "a real aristocracy, armed with a perfected science and working to a logical conclusion the industrial system of today." But again the reader is warned that the interpretation may be mistaken: "This, I must warn you, was my theory at the time. . . . My explanation may be absolutely wrong" (50).

Having descended into the subterranean world of the Morlocks, the storyteller modifies his hypothesis yet again. Now he is convinced that it is the Morlocks who are the dominant species and that they are simply biding their time before returning to the surface and claiming their birthright. Later still comes the chilling realization that the truth is even more horrible, that the Eloi are merely cattle for the carnivorous Morlocks and that the decadent aristocracy with which the Time Traveler has identified himself live in terror of their loathsome persecutors. Even at this stage a note of doubt is introduced: "It may be as wrong an explanation as mortal wit could invent. It is how the thing shaped itself to me, and as that I give it to you."

The device employed by the Time Traveler, then, is one of continually teasing the reader—expectations are built up only to be demolished. *The Time Machine* is characteristic of modernist texts, in that none of the reader's assumptions are fulfilled: society is not based on harmony but on conflict, Weena is destroyed not by the Morlocks but in the fire lit by the Traveler himself, the Traveler disappears at the end of the story never to return. In each case the expectations so carefully built up by the narrator are overturned.

An interesting example of the author toying with the reader becomes apparent when we try to establish the "narrative present" of the story—when did the events described in the opening and closing chapters take place? We can infer from the date of the lecture by Simon Newcomb referred to at the beginning of the narrative that the conversation recounted in the first chapter takes place in the spring of 1894. The dinner when the Traveler reappears after his time traveling adventures takes place one week later. Yet Hillyer tells us at the end of chapter 12 that the Traveler vanished "three years ago." Three years *after* 1894 gives us a date of 1897 as the "narrative present." Bearing in mind that the story was published as a serial in 1894, this means that Wells is deliberately placing the story *in the future*. It could, of course, be argued that this is simply a slip on Wells's part, but is it not much more likely that this is a deliberate device and entirely characteristic of the author in his scientific romances and short stories? Toying with the reader in this way is a typical Wellsian device, one he employs to great effect in such tales as "The Plattner Story," "The Late Mr Elvesham," and "The Man Who Could Work Miracles." In his world nothing can be taken for granted.

IMAGERY

The Time Machine is a text unusually rich in imagery: masculine/feminine, conscious/unconscious, classical/romantic. It is worth exploring some of these elements in detail in order to highlight its significance as a seminal novel in the history of science fiction.

Masculine/feminine imagery is evident, for example, in the repeated references to the sun and the moon (the sun is a male symbol, representing the male ego, while the moon is traditionally a feminine image, associated with the anima). Weena is often referred to in the context of the moon: "The little people were sleeping in the moonlight—that night Weena was among them," and it is Weena who first alerts the Traveler to the dangers associated with the waning moon: "The enemy I dreaded may surprise you. It was the darkness of the new moon. Weena had put this into my head" (57).

The moon is a well known feminine symbol, associated with passivity, the imagination, and the unconscious. In contrast, references to the sun in *The Time Machine* are associated with masculine imagery: a thunderstorm (his arrival in 802,701), heat (the hotter sun in the "Golden Age"), conflict (the final struggle with the Morlocks). The contrast between the two reflects the dichotomy within the Traveler's own temperament between the gentler qualities of affection and compassion, and the more masculine traits of courage and strength.

One of the most potent images in the novel is that of the sphinx. The first edition of the novel has a sphinx embossed on the cover, as if to emphasize its central importance. The sphinx is an implicit challenge to both the narrator and the reader. What, it seems to ask, is the meaning of the story? Behind this lies a larger question: what is the meaning of the riddle of life? Few readers can forget the haunting description of the first sight of the sphinx:

> My sensations would be hard to describe. As the columns of hail grew thinner, I saw the white figure more distinctly. It was very large, for a silver birch-tree touched its shoulder. It was of white marble, in shape something like a winged sphinx, but the wings, instead of being carried vertically at the sides, were spread so that it seemed to hover. The pedestal, it appeared to me, was of bronze, and was thick with verdigris. It chanced that the face was towards me; the sightless eyes seemed to watch me; there was the faint shadow of a smile on the lips. It was greatly weather-worn, and that imparted an unpleasant suggestion of disease (21).

Note the proliferation of words suggesting decay: "verdigris," "sightless," "shadow," "weather-worn," "disease." This figure seems to watch him through all his subsequent explorations:

> And so I was led past the sphinx of white marble, which had seemed to watch me all the while with a smile at my astonishment, towards a vast grey edifice of fretted stone (25).
>
> Above me towered the sphinx upon the bronze pedestal, white, shining, leprous, in the light of the rising moon. It seemed to smile in mockery of my dismay (35).

The narrator senses instinctively that the sphinx, with its watching eyes and "faint shadow of a smile on its lips," contains the clue to this strange world. It seems to mock him, to challenge him with the unspoken riddle: what does this world mean?

J. E. Cirlot, in *A Dictionary of Symbols,* states that "being the supreme embodiment of the enigma, the sphinx keeps watch over an ultimate meaning that must remain for ever beyond the understanding of man."[1] The fact that the statue is winged and seems to hover heightens its power as a symbol that broods over the novel, an inscrutable mystery.

The enigmatic smile on the face of the sphinx seems to mock the Traveler, yet he senses that in some way it offers a clue to the puzzle. As he expresses it, "I felt I lacked a clue. I felt—how shall I put it? Suppose you found an inscription, with sentences here and there in excellent plain English, and, interpolated therewith, others made up of words, of letters even, absolutely unknown to you?" (42).

The image of a partially deciphered text is a fitting metaphor for his bafflement. It is clear that the statue of the marble sphinx is meant to convey a meaning, but what that meaning is remains unclear.

The sphinx is his first sight of the world of 802,701, but it is also his last. From beginning to end it fails to give up its secrets. Note also that his first glimpse of it is indistinct, through a hailstorm, when "all else of the world was invisible." Solve the riddle of the sphinx, it seems to be saying, before embarking on your journey. It is an implicit challenge to solve the riddle of life.

As he gazes at the statue he is smitten with doubts as to the wisdom of his journey: "I looked up again at the crouching white shape, and the full temerity of my voyage came suddenly upon me" (22). In this sense the sphinx is the central image of the novel. Because it suggests a mask, a symbol of unfathomable mystery, it seems to brood over the story, always present in the background. It is the key to the story—symbolically because it poses a mystery, and literally because for much of his stay the Time Machine is concealed within it. By combining masculine and feminine elements (the head and body of a lion and the wings of a bird) the sphinx embodies symbols of both strength and imagination. It represents the two qualities most needed by the Traveler on his journey: physical courage and mental aspiration.

The narrator stresses that the eyes of the sphinx are "sightless." It poses many questions, but it cannot itself offer any solution to the mystery. However, though the sphinx is silent the reader can share vicariously with the Traveler in the unraveling of the riddle—he can journey on through time, offering tantalizing glimpses of the future of mankind. But in place of confident assumptions of material and moral progress, Wells offers a vision of man as a doomed species, a race driven by fear and internecine hatreds.

A further strand interwoven with the narrative is a complex substructure of religious imagery. The description of the Traveler's arrival in a beautiful garden can be read as a parody of the biblical account of paradise: "The air was free from gnats, the earth from weeds or fungi; everywhere were fruits and sweet and delightful flowers; brilliant butterflies flew hither and thither" (32). Almost his first act on reaching the world of 802,701 is to eat a meal of fruit, a reflection of the biblical story of the Garden of Eden and the Fall of Man. The vivid account of the Morlocks in their underground cavern closely resembles the picture of hell and its demons Wells had seen as a child in his mother's copy of Sturm's *Reflections*. (As we have seen, his mother had done her utmost to instill into him her rigid theology, with its literal belief in the devil and the netherworld. The Morlocks, "these unpleasant creatures from below, these whitened Lemurs," can be seen as a personification of these childhood terrors.) The "faint halitus of freshly-shed blood" in the Morlocks cavern is clearly a reflection of the Christian emphasis on a blood sacrifice, while the "little table of white metal, laid with what seemed a meal" is a grotesque parody of the sacrament. Most striking of all is the unforgettable description of the forest fire with its vivid evocation of hell:

> And now I was to see the most weird and horrible thing, I think, of all that I beheld in that future age. This whole space was as bright as day with the reflection of the fire. . . . For the most part of that night I was persuaded it was a nightmare. I bit myself and screamed in a passionate desire to awake. . . . Then I would fall to rubbing my eyes and calling upon God to let me awake. Thrice

> I saw Morlocks put their heads down in a kind of agony and rush into the flames (75–76).

Demonic and paradisal imagery forms a significant element within the story and is a further reminder of Wells's lifelong debt to Swift. In writing his first novel he was expressing in the form of a myth his deepest intuitions concerning man, and simultaneously creating a secular version of Eden. In this sense the story is an inversion of the doctrine of the Fall. In place of the notion that man has regressed from his former exalted state, *The Time Machine* presents the opposite view—that man will regress into two species—one effete, indolent, decadent; the other brutish, inhuman, malign. In this bleak vision regression is a prospect for the future not the past.

The landscape of *The Time Machine* frequently resembles that seen in a dream:

> So far as I could see, all the world displayed the same exuberant richness as the Thames valley. From every hill I climbed I saw the same abundance of splendid buildings, endlessly varied in material and style, the same clustering thickets of evergreens, the same blossom-laden trees and tree-ferns. Here and there water shone like silver, and beyond, the land rose into blue undulating hills, and so faded into the serenity of the sky (40).

It is worth paying careful attention to the language and imagery of Wells's description. Note the juxtaposition of "clustering thickets of evergreens" and "blossom-laden trees." Evergreens symbolize the *everlasting* side of life, all that endures. *Blossom,* in contrast, is transitory. The presence of both abundant evergreens and blossoms symbolizes the passage of time.

The reference to blossom is a reminder of the Traveler's arrival in 802,701, when the Eloi heap flowers upon him, and neatly prefigures the novel's closing image of the "two strange white flowers" that are such a poignant reminder of his love for Weena. His story begins and ends with flowers, for his first sight of the future world is of blossoms dropping to the ground under a shower of hailstones. It is fitting that the image is a feminine one, a further reminder of the contrasting masculine/feminine imagery that is so prominent a theme in Wells's fiction.

The water shining "like silver" is a frequently recurring image in folklore. Silver in the language of symbols represents illumination and wisdom. It is also a feminine image. Crucially, his sight of the shining river occurs just before his first encounter with Weena, symbolizing his unconscious desire for the feminine, intuitive elements in his nature. The "blue undulating hills" represent the difficulties and obstacles he still has to surmount. His description of the landscape occurs at an early stage in the narrative, when he still has to face a whole series of trials—his first sight of the Morlocks, his descent down the well, the arduous journey to the Palace of Green Porcelain, the struggle in the forest, his escape from the clutches of the Morlocks. The hills symbolize this travail, but note that at last the scenery "faded into the serenity of the sky." There is a hint here that ultimately he will triumph over all the obstacles placed in his path.

The Time Machine begins in light but ends in darkness. In the opening chapter there are references to "shone," "twinkled," "burned brightly," "radiance," "incandescent," "bright light," "brilliantly illuminated." When the novel ends thirty million years hence, Wells's language is suffused with the language of twilight: "dim," "inky," "blackness," "darkling," "sunset," "obscurity." The contrast between the brilliant light of the opening and the impenetrable darkness of the end could not be more marked. It is the contrast between the optimism of the beginning of the journey (the Time Traveler setting out on his voyage of exploration) and the pessimism of the conclusion (the Traveler witnessing the demise of civilization and the end of man).

CLASSICAL AND ROMANTIC

In the Traveler's attraction toward Weena we find an interesting example of the divided self. As a man of science he is well aware that dalliance with feminine companionship forms no part of his plans; it is his business to learn all he can of future civilization, regardless of distractions. "But the problems of the world had to be mastered," he observes, "I had not, I said to myself, come into the future to carry on a miniature flirtation." (43). Rationally, he is fully conscious of this; yet emotionally, he is powerfully drawn: "Yet her distress when I left her was very great, her expostulations at the parting were sometimes frantic, and I think, altogether, I had as much trouble as comfort from her devotion." She heaps blossoms upon him, comforts him with affection, and on his return to his own time he finds his pockets filled with flowers she has placed there. This emotional, sentimental side of his temperament is in the sharpest contrast to the image of the dispassionate man of reason he has been so careful to cultivate since the outset of the story.

Though he is at pains to record as accurately as possible his impressions of the world about him, his response is frequently expressed in romantic terms. He states that "everywhere were fruits and sweet and delightful flowers; brilliant butterflies flew hither and thither." He refers to "beautiful pagoda-like plants," a prospect that was "as sweet and fair a view as I have ever seen." In describing the sunset on his first day he observes that "the sun had already gone below the horizon and the west was flaming gold, touched with some horizontal bars of purple and crimson." He is beckoned by the "tall pinnacles" of the Palace of Green Porcelain (itself a romantic concept) and is comforted by the beauty of the starlit sky. Again and again he refers to the beauty of flowers and blossoms, the effects of light and shadow on landscape and buildings, the wonder of moon and stars. These are not the reactions one would associate with a rational man of science, but they are characteristic of Wells in his novels and short stories. (In an article written at the same time the novel was being composed, "The Degeneration of the Ravensbourne," Wells wrote touchingly of the despoliation of the countryside around Bromley, a countryside he had come to know and love as a child.)[2] *The Time Machine* is the work of a man who is determined to establish his scientific credentials and yet is simultaneously drawn to visions of beauty and desire.

The dichotomy is symbolized at numerous points in the narrative, most strikingly in the journey toward the Palace of Green Porcelain, when the Traveler is confronted by a river: "So we went down a long slope into a valley, and there in the dimness I almost walked into a little river. This I waded, and went up the opposite side of the valley, past a number of sleeping-houses, and by a statue—a Faun, or some such figure, minus the head. Here, too, were acacias" (60).

This passage is rich in symbolism, neatly encapsulating his journey. In psychological terms a valley is a symbol for the feminine realm, representing the softer, gentler aspects of his nature, which he must acknowledge if he is to be true to himself. Crossing a river is a metaphor for surmounting an obstacle in order to reach the other side, as the Traveler does when he outwits the Morlocks and retrieves the Time Machine. A faun in classical mythology is a pastoral image, symbolizing nature and fertility. The fact that the statue lacks its head suggests a flawed paradise. Acacias are a traditional representation of life and rebirth; in ancient Egypt they were also symbols of knowledge and initiation.

In summary, then, the descent into the valley and the crossing of the river are echoes of his encounter with Weena and the overcoming of the obstacles placed in his path. The faun is a reminder of the flawed Eden of the Eloi; it is a beautiful world tarnished by decay (the phrase *minus the head* also suggests a lack of intelligence). Finally the acacias are a reminder of the Traveler's ultimate victory—equipped with knowledge he eventually triumphs over the Morlocks and escapes from his own death. As a rational being, he knows he has to cross the river in order to reach his goal. As an emotional being, he is aware of drives pulling him in the opposite direction—toward Weena and his romantic desires. (The sleeping-houses he passes in the valley are an echo of the Sleeping Beauty legend, which is present in the background for much of the story).

It can be seen that *The Time Machine* is a story built upon a pattern of opposites:

masculine—feminine
rational—emotional
darkness—light
classical—romantic.

In the contrast and interplay between these opposites lies much of the tension implicit in the narrative.

IRONY

Wells frequently employs irony as a literary device, most notably in *The Island of Dr. Moreau* (1896) and *The First Men in the Moon* (1901), both of which can be regarded as ironic fables. Irony is also evident in his first novel.

An example of this can be seen in the Traveler's ambivalent attitude to the eating of meat. At several points in the narrative he condemns the Morlocks for their liking for human meat, but he himself is eager to eat animal meat as soon as he returns to his home. "I'm starving for a bit of meat," he announces, "what a treat it is to stick a fork into meat again," "I sniffed good wholesome meat." The reader is invited to feel disgust and horror at the cannibalism of the Morlocks, and yet the narrator admits his own partiality for meat.

A more fundamental example is apparent in the Traveler's attitude to the Morlocks, who are portrayed throughout as inhuman. He refers to them as "sickening," "inhuman," and "malign" (57), and he admits that he loathed them instinctively. The reader is encouraged to share his attitude of repugnance:

> I rejoined her with a mace in my hand more than sufficient, I judged, for any Morlock skull I might encounter. And I longed very much to kill a Morlock or so. Very inhuman, you may think, to want to go killing one's own descendants! But it was impossible, somehow, to feel any humanity in the things (67).

It has to be remembered that *The Time Machine* was written at a time of the apogee of empire. The British Empire was at its height; there was much talk of "inferior races," "subject peoples," and "the white man's burden." The repugnance and fear that the Eloi feel for the Morlocks can be seen as an ironic representation of prevalent attitudes toward nonwhite races. Again and again the narrator describes the Morlocks in terms that are calculated to arouse distaste: the adjectives used to portray them are "ape-like," "human spider," "bleached," "obscene," "pallid," "dreadful," "nauseating," "human rats." Many readers in the 1890s would not have recognized the description as an encapsulation of their own attitudes, yet Wells's use of irony here is powerfully effective. The point is made explicit in *The War of the Worlds,* where the narrator urges the reader not to condemn the Martians too readily but to remember that "the Tasmanians, in spite of their human likeness, were entirely swept out of existence in a war of extermination waged by European immigrants, in a space of fifty years."[3] The intolerance of many people toward the "inferior races" is echoed in the attitude of the Eloi toward the Morlocks, and in the Traveler's own violent distaste. His emotional, instinctive reaction is in marked contrast to his professed rationality as a dispassionate man of science.

In this connection Wells's repeated stress on the word "white" is interesting: "white stone," "white figure," "white marble." The image of the white sphinx, diseased and weather-worn, is a potent symbol of the decline of white imperialism—a remarkably prescient image in a book written at the climax of the Victorian age: "But, clearly, the old order was already in part reversed. The Nemesis of the delicate ones was creeping on apace. Ages ago, thousands of generations ago, man had thrust his brother man out of the ease and the sunshine. And now that brother was coming back—changed!" (58).

Whether one sees this as an anticipation of the end of empire or the end of the old order exemplified by Uppark, it remains a remarkably accurate forecast and a recurring theme throughout his fiction and sociological writings.

Irony is also evident in the passages where the Traveler thinks aloud about the nature of society. A case in point is a passage following his descent into the well: "I came out of this age of ours, this ripe prime of the human race, when Fear does not paralyse and Mystery has lost its terrors" (58). He is being heavily sarcastic at his own expense, for we know from his own statements that he was smitten with fear while he was down the well—"I will confess I was horribly frightened"—and distressed by the mystery of unknown dangers. We also know that he does not regard the 1890s as the "ripe prime of the human race" but that on the contrary, as Hillyer tells us in the epilogue, he thought the steady accumulation of material progress was "only a foolish heaping that must inevitably fall back upon and destroy its makers in the end."

An element of irony is also present in the Traveler's account of himself. For all his pretensions as a man of culture—he tells us he is a contributor to *Philosophical Transactions* and the author of a series of papers on physical optics—he is prone to fits of violence and anger. He admits to "the strange exultation that so often seems to accompany hard fighting" and boasts that when fighting the Morlocks "I could feel the succulent giving of flesh and bone under my blows" (74). His veneer of civilization and reason gives way to brute force and sheer animality when confronted with his foes. He admits that he "struck furiously at them with my bar, in a frenzy of fear." His public persona as a respected scientist and author is belied at times by his totally irrational behavior and attitudes.

Throughout his narrative a dual process is in operation. He is telling his story aloud to a group of largely skeptical listeners. At a later stage the reader is following the story that Hillyer has written down. The Traveler cannot see himself from the outside, but his audience can, and so too does the reader. Since the reader, unlike the Traveler's guests, has the whole narrative before him and can study it at leisure, he is in a better position to assess the Traveler's character and behavior. We can see the Traveler for what he is—a fallible human being with the normal complement of anger, fear, hatred, and violence. For all his claims to be a man of science, he embodies in his own person the strengths and weaknesses of human nature. In this respect he is totally removed from the calm, wholly rational protagonists of other futuristic romances. Compare, for example, Leete in Bellamy's *Looking Backward* or Frazier in B. F. Skinner's *Walden Two,* neither of whom seem to have human frailties.

THE DERELICT MUSEUM

At the thematic heart of the novel is the account of the Traveler and Weena journeying through Surrey to the Palace of Green Porcelain, and the description of all that they find there. His first sight of the palace occurs midway through the story, when he sees far off "a vast green structure, different in character from any I had hitherto seen" (52). From this point onward the building becomes a goal he is eager to explore. He is attracted by its tall pinnacles and bluish-green color; he literally looks up to it for "it lay very high upon a turfy down." If the structure of the novel can be represented diagrammatically as a pyramid, the bottom left-hand corner is the descent into the well, the bottom right-hand point is the trap of the White Sphinx, and the apex of the triangle is the Palace of Green Porcelain. Both structurally and thematically it forms the high point of the novel, the summit that the Traveler must reach if he is to attain his goal.

The image of a derelict museum is peculiarly apposite in the context of the story, for as he wanders through the dust-laden galleries and exhibits he is seeing all human achievement in review. He walks slowly through the galleries—palaeontology, mineralogy, natural history, technology, chemistry, and a library—musing on human destiny and the fate that has overtaken science and culture. The extremely dilapidated state of the building and its contents symbolizes the precarious nature of civilization. The building is "deserted and falling into ruin," the museum is "thick with dust," the library has crumbled into "brown and charred rags." Standing in the center of the entrance hall are the skeletons of extinct creatures, including a megatherium and a brontosaurus. The implication is clear: *Homo sapiens* is doomed to join these creatures in extinction. The inference is that it is not simply man's inventions that are things of the past but man himself. This is reinforced by a footnote added by Wells suggesting that the museum was built into the side of a hill, thus recalling the tombs and burial chambers of prehistory. The museum becomes a metaphor for the death of civilization.

There are many machines and exhibits in the museum, but there is no mention of another time machine. Clearly, then, neither the Morlocks nor anyone else has been able to replicate the Traveler's invention. This is a further reminder of the central importance of this episode. His only means of escaping from 802,701 and returning to his own time is either to find his original machine or build a replica himself; he has no other alternative. The journey to the Palace of Green Porcelain is thus crucial to his mission in both a literal and symbolic sense. His exploration of the museum confirms beyond doubt that science and literature have come to an end. It also establishes the fact that the invention of a machine that can travel through time is an invention peculiar to himself. From this point onward he is equipped with a new resolve to face the Morlocks.

Before leaving the Palace of Green Porcelain the Traveler and Weena find a resting place in an open space: "It was after that, I think, that we came to a little open court within the palace. It was turfed, and had three fruit-trees. So we rested and refreshed ourselves." In psychological terms a courtyard represents a place of seclusion and safety, in contrast to the region of danger and fear outside. The three fruit trees are another image of time, symbolizing past, present, and future. The Traveler is now at a turning point in his adventures—after surmounting many difficulties he has journeyed to the palace, found a weapon with which to face his adversaries, and is now entering the decisive phase. He has reached a stage when he can pause and rest.

The image of the open courtyard appears again in his story "The Door in the Wall" (1906), where there is a reference to a palace containing "a grass-covered court where there was a sundial set about with flowers."[4] The "grass-covered court" that occurs in both stories is an apt metaphor for the unconscious, the center of the Traveler's imaginative life. The court itself is an open space, but it is enclosed "within the palace"; it forms the literal center of his exploration of the palace and the symbolic center of his narrative. Always one is reminded of time, of the transience of things. The court is covered in grass, symbolizing the encroachment of nature. At the center of his mental life he is still subject to the remorseless passage of time.

THE SIGNIFICANCE OF WEENA

From adolescence onward Wells had been beckoned by a vision of "a lovely, wise and generous person wholly devoted to me. Her embraces were to be my sure fastness, my ultimate reassurance, the culmination of my realisation of myself."[5] This fixation, which he termed "the goddess" complex, haunted him throughout his life—a vision of a perfect loveliness of feminine response.[6] This is the Anima figure, the female shadow figure in the male psyche, that haunts so much of his fiction including the short stories "The Door in the Wall" and "Mr Skelmersdale in Fairyland," and the novels *The Sea Lady* and *Tono-Bungay*. In the figure of Weena in *The Time Machine* we have one of the earliest examples in his fiction of this motif. She is described as a "little doll of a creature," entirely dependent on him. Because she follows him "exactly like a child" and showers him with affection, he finds her presence comforting and reassuring, until at last she gives his return to the neighborhood of the sphinx "almost the feeling of coming home." Unlike other members of the Eloi he has met, Weena displays qualities of gratitude, tenderness, and loyalty that he finds appealing; he is so drawn to her that he resolves to bring her back with him to his own time. It is easy to understand why the Traveler should become so attracted toward her. Alone and friendless in an inhospitable world, he sees embodied in her possibilities of companionship and affection he cannot find elsewhere. In her diminutive figure there are unmistakeable echoes of Wells's wife, Amy Catherine Robbins, who was devoted to Wells as steadfastly as Weena to the Time Traveler. But beyond this she has psychological significance as a symbol of the Anima, the reassuring presence who comforts and consoles. She is first seen drowning in a river, an image recurring in almost identical form in Wells's dystopia *Mr. Blettsworthy on Rampole Island* (1928), in which the narrator rescues a girl, Rowena, from drowning. Water is a well-known symbol of the Anima, recalling Diana in the Actaeon myth. All Wells's life was a search for a mother-figure, the woman who is at once passionate and gentle, loving and protective. "I returned to the welcome and the caresses of little Weena," writes the Traveler. "she was a very great comfort. . . . Nor until it was too late did I clearly understand what she was to me" (43–44). With her demise he feels terribly alone, cut off from human companionship and emotion.

In *The Early H. G. Wells,* Bernard Bergonzi finds the Time Traveler's dalliance with Weena "the biggest flaw in the narrative, for it is totally unconvincing," while V. S. Pritchett in a celebrated passage describes their relationship as "faint squirms of idyllic petting."[7] But it can be argued that on the contrary, the Traveler's love affair with Weena is an episode of central importance to *The Time Machine* and one rich in psychological significance.

In the light of Jungian psychology, Weena can be seen as a characteristic Anima figure. She is rescued from drowning; she is described as a "tiny figure of white and gold" (the color white, because of its association with the moon, is often associated with symbols of the Anima); she has to be awakened from sleep ("she seemed scarcely to breathe"); the Traveler has to overcome a series of obstacles and dangers in his attempts to rescue her from the Morlocks.

Throughout his life, as we have just noted, Wells's imagination was haunted by this goddess figure, by the beautiful, alluring female who would beckon and embrace. As he expressed it in his autobiography, from the age of seven onward he was fascinated by "nameless goddess mistresses of which I never breathed a word to any human being."[8]

The relationship between Weena and the Traveler cannot simply be dismissed as sentimental. At first he is grateful to her for assuaging his loneliness. "For, by merely seeming fond of me, and showing in her weak futile way that she cared for me, the little doll of a creature presently gave my return to the neighborhood of the White Sphinx almost the feeling of coming home" (44). Gradually their relationship deepens until when at last she dies he is overwhelmed with grief: "I felt the intensest wretchedness for the horrible death of little Weena.

It seemed an overwhelming calamity. Now, in this old familiar room, it is more like the sorrow of a dream than an actual loss. But that morning it left me absolutely lonely again—terribly alone" (77). It is Weena who sustains him through most of his sojourn in the world of 802,701 by her companionship and devotion to him; it is Weena who accompanies him on his journey to the Palace of Green Porcelain (corresponding to the enchanted castle of fairy tales); it is she who is at his side during his crucial encounter with the Morlocks in the forest; and it is she who, by her gift of flowers, convinces the narrator that "gratitude and a mutual tenderness still lived on in the heart of man" (91).

Weena therefore plays a central role in the narrative, for it is she, alone of all the Eloi, who engages the Time Traveler's feelings. Her loyalty and tenderness are such that instead of dismissing the Eloi as irredeemably worthless, he has to acknowledge the over-hastiness of his judgments: "I had got to such a low estimate of her kind that I did not expect any gratitude from her. In that, however, I was wrong" (43). In providing him with companionship and solace Weena evokes a reciprocal response from the Traveler and thus provides the narrative with a human perspective it would otherwise lack. In contrast to the anonymity of the effete Eloi and the repellent Morlocks, Weena stands out precisely because of her human qualities.

Without Weena *The Time Machine* would still be a gripping narrative and a vividly written account of a journey through time. But with Weena it is a haunting depiction of a quest—a quest to free the sleeping princess of legend from the clutches of her pursuers. In rescuing Weena from drowning, befriending her, taking her side against her enemies and journeying with her across a landscape beset with dangers and obstacles, the Traveler calls upon all his resources of strength and intelligence. Beyond this, despite his inclination to regard himself as a skeptical man of science, he is forced to acknowledge the presence within his own makeup of feelings of tenderness and compassion. This adds a humane perspective to *The Time Machine* and enhances its power as an allegory of the human adventure.

THE NATURE OF TIME

Time is an important element in any novel. It is doubly important in *The Time Machine,* for the novel is both an ingenious speculation on the nature of time and a metaphor of the slow but inevitable death of the universe.

Part of the background to the writing and publication of *The Time Machine* was renewed discussion concerning the nature of time itself.

It was only in 1884, ten years before its writing, that time had been standardized throughout the world and international time zones based on the Greenwich meridian had been established. In locating the home of the Time Traveler at Richmond, a few miles from Greenwich, Wells was not simply placing the action of the story in a desirable part of London but locating it *close to the center of time*. Greenwich Mean Time was the standard by which time was measured throughout the earth. By the same token, a traveler embarking on a journey through time from this location would be symbolically and actually near to the focal point of the time dimension.

While reading the novel one is continually aware of the passage of time. There are frequent reminders of day and night; the text is littered with such words as "sunset," "evening," "night," "moonlight," "darkness," "dawn." Always in the background is an awareness of time as a dominant presence. This is underlined by the numerous references to clocks and watches:

> The thing the Time Traveler held in his hand was a glittering metallic framework, scarcely larger than a small clock, and very delicately made (8).
>
> It was at ten o'clock today that the first of all Time Machines began its career (18).
>
> I found that the thousands hand was sweeping round as fast as the seconds hand of a watch—into futurity (81).
>
> I found the date was indeed today, and looking at the timepiece, saw that the hour was almost eight o'clock (86).
>
> The Journalist fumbled for his watch (87).
>
> I looked at my watch, and saw that I could barely save that engagement (90).

The cumulative effect is to reinforce in the mind of the reader a consciousness of time and duration. Beyond this, Wells is keen to draw an analogy between clockwork and the motion of the universe; the passing of time represented by the hands on the clock becomes a metaphor for the inexorable running down of the solar cycle: "I thought of the great precessional cycle that the pole of the earth describes. Only forty times had that silent revolution occurred during all the years that I had traversed" (61).

The sense of a universe gradually slowing down is hauntingly expressed in the final chapter, with the insistent reiteration of such words as "slower," "drag," "twilight," "creeping," "motionless." The reader has a sense of the gradual winding down of a clock. As the Traveler journeys farther and farther into the future, he approaches closer and closer to solar death.

The contrast between the two journeys into the future enhances this impression. The journey toward 802,701 is characterized by such terms as "headlong," "helpless," "twinkling," "exhilaration." The journey into the more distant future, on the other hand, is described in terms suggesting a marked slowing down: "cautiously," "slower," "gently," "halted," "reverse." The language of acceleration is replaced by the language of retardation.

From this perspective the novel is not only a history of the future but also a chilling parable on the theme of the end of time. Both the Traveler and the reader know that just as day follows night with relentless inevitability, so a day will come when the solar system in which our planet revolves will cease to be.

POETIC VISION

We have previously drawn attention to the significance of *The Time Machine* as a parable symbolizing man's journey through the evolutionary cycle, his beginnings as a neophyte, his struggle against the forces of darkness and ignorance, and final extinction. The poetic quality of the vision of the earth in the distant future is intense in its power. Like Crusoe's sight of the footprint in the sand or the first glimpse of Treasure Island, it is one of those images that haunt the imagination:

> So I travelled, stopping ever and again, in great strides of a thousand years or more, drawn on by the mystery of the earth's fate, watching with a strange fascination the sun grow larger and duller in the westward sky, and the life of the old earth ebb away. . . . A bitter cold assailed me. Rare white flakes ever and again came eddying down. To the north-eastward, the glare of snow lay under the starlight of the sable sky, and I could see an undulating crest of hillocks pinkish white. There were fringes of ice along the sea margin, with drifting masses further out; but the main expanse of that salt ocean, all bloody under the eternal sunset, was still unfrozen (83–84).

There is a sense of man, utterly alone, witnessing the slow decline of his planet. It is as if the Traveler is a camera dispassionately recording the end of the earth; he watches in silence while all around him is evidence of terminal decline. The reiterated imagery of coldness is memorable in its impact: "flecked with white," "bitter cold," "rare white flakes," "fringes of ice." In his essay "On Extinction" he had written eloquently of the tragedy of extinction, reminding his readers that "in the long galleries of the geological museum are the records of judgments that have been passed graven upon the rocks." He continued: "Surely a chill of solitude must strike to the heart of the last stragglers in the rout, the last survivors of the defeated and vanishing species. . . . The sunniest day must shine with a cold and desert light on the eyes of the condemned. For them the future is blotted out, and hope is vanity."[9] Now in the closing pages of *The Time Machine* he gives imaginative expression to this vision, depicting in a series of indelible images the slow degeneration of a dying world. No one who reads this description can ever forget the impression of coldness, silence, darkness, and death. The sense of that "remote and awful twilight" remains in the consciousness long after the book has been put down. The total effect is chilling in its power; it will take its place as one of the most memorable scenes in English literature.

"I cannot convey the sense of abominable desolation that hung over the world," says the Traveler. The haunting description of the desolate beach is etched into the mind through an accumulation of imagery: the dying sun, the thin air, the cold wind, the gathering darkness, the eerie silence. Whether one sees this as an anticipation of the death of the planet or as an echo of Isaiah's prediction: "Until cities lie waste without inhabitants, and houses without men, and the land is utterly desolate," there is no denying its impact.[10] Through his long literary career Wells never surpassed this haunting vision.

THE TIME MACHINE AS A FIRST NOVEL

The question arises: Why did Wells take such pains over the writing of the story? It is not unusual for a first novel to be carefully written, but *The Time Machine* is remarkable in being written with such elaborate care over so long a period. Wells clearly felt a deep intellectual and emotional attachment to the story—we have already seen that he referred to it as "my trump card" and "my peculiar treasure"—and sensed it was an idea that would either make or break his career. Beyond this, the meticulous care with which he worked on a succession of drafts over a period of eight years is an indication of the seriousness of his literary ambitions and his desire to create a work of enduring merit. There is a telling moment in the derelict museum when the Traveler, seeing the decayed remnants of books, reflects on the mortality of literary attainment: "Had I been a literary man I might, perhaps, have moralised upon the futility of all ambition. But as it was, the thing that struck me with keenest force was the enormous waste of labour to which this sombre wilderness of rotting paper testified" (68).

It is not difficult to see in this passage the young author speculating on his own future and wondering whether all his efforts would be in vain. He could not have known then that the novel would itself become a kind of Time Machine, carrying his name into futurity. *The Time Machine* is not only the story of the Traveler and his journey into the future; it is the story of a little-known writer launching his first novel on to the world.

There remains the further question: What kind of book is it, to what genre does it belong? Is it a novel, a romance, or science fiction? It has come to be regarded as science fiction, and indeed paperback editions frequently describe it as "the brilliant forerunner of today's science fiction." But the label does not fit comfortably, for in fact the book contains very little science per se. My own reading would suggest that *romance* is a more accurate term to describe it. Wells himself felt that *The Time Machine* was an exercise of the imagination in a totally different field from the works of Jules Verne, that it belonged to a genre of writing "which includes the *Golden Ass* of Apuleius, the *True Histories of Lucian, Peter Schlemil* and the story of *Frankenstein.*" He continued: "They are all fantasies; they do not aim to project a serious possibility; they aim indeed only at the same amount of conviction as one gets in a good gripping dream."[11]

In an early version of the story Wells has the Time Traveler say to his audience, "Assume it is all a fable. Let me tell it as a story I have invented. Don't call me a liar but a fabulist."[12] In answer to the question of what manner of work *The Time Machine* is, we are surely justified in answering that it is an exercise of the imagination, a fable or romance after the manner of *Gulliver's Travels* or *Robinson Crusoe*. In depicting the Traveler's journey into the distant future Wells created a myth of enduring relevance and at the same time one that is deeply rooted in his own psychology. All his work from *The Time Machine* to the apocalyptic writings of his final years is characterized by a duality between rational, scientific elements, on the one hand, and emotional, symbolic elements, on the other. His first full-length narrative presents this contrast in an acute form by pitting a nineteenth-century man of science against the forces of darkness and evil. Moreover, it embodies themes that remained emblematic of his work throughout his literary career: the rise and death of the Anima figure, the image of a lost paradise and an enchanted garden, the quest for beauty that beckons and eludes. He was to return to these themes in *The Sea Lady,*

The History of Mr Polly, "The Country of the Blind," and many other stories, but their presence can be detected in his earliest work.

In a number of respects *The Time Machine* marks a watershed in the coming of modernism. It predates Conrad's *Heart of Darkness* (1899), an equally seminal text that owes much to Wells's sombre vision, and it anticipates many of the literary devices employed by twentieth-century modernists. While the opening chapters appear to place it in the tradition of "an imaginative romance stamped with many characteristics of the Stevenson and early Kipling period in which it was written,"[13] it soon becomes apparent that it marks a major departure from the conventions of the late Victorian romance. In its deliberate toying with the expectations of the reader, its absence of authorial omniscience, its extensive use of symbolism, and its ambiguous ending, it consciously rejects the norms of its time and looks ahead to such writers as Kafka and Golding. In implicitly questioning man's domination, the novel not only flies in the face of the utopian speculations of the age; it is an important precursor of a new genre of "dystopias," including his own *When the Sleeper Wakes* (1899). In his first novel Wells created a myth imbued with the dilemmas and uncertainties of the modern age.

NOTES

1. J. E. Cirlot, *A Dictionary of Symbols* (London: Routledge and Kegan Paul, 1981), 304.
2. "The Degeneration of the Ravensbourne," *Pall Mall Gazette,* 12 July 1894.
3. Wells, *The War of the Worlds* (Heinemann, 1898), book 1, chap. 1.
4. Wells, "The Door in the Wall," in *The Country of the Blind and Other Stories* (London: Nelson, 1911), and also in *The Complete Short Stories of H. G. Wells* (London: Dent, 1998).
5. Wells, *H. G. Wells in Love,* ed. by G. P. Wells (London: Faber and Faber, 1984), 56.
6. Wells, *Experiment in Autobiography* (London: Gollancz, 1934), 79–82.
7. Bergonzi, *The Early H. G. Wells* (Manchester: Manchester University Press, 1961), 50; V. S. Pritchett, *The Living Novel* (London: Chatto and Windus, 1946), 119.
8. Wells, *Experiment in Autobiography,* 82.
9. Wells, "On Extinction," *Chambers Journal,* 30 September 1893, 623–24, in Robert Philmus and David Y. Hughes, eds., *H. G. Wells: Early Writings in Science and Science Fiction* (Berkeley: University of California Press, 1975), 169–72.
10. Isaiah 6: 11.
11. Wells, preface to *The Scientific Romances of H. G. Wells* (London:

Gollancz, 1933), included in *H. G. Wells's Literary Criticism*, ed. Patrick Parrinder and Robert Philmus (London: Harvester, 1980), 240–44.

12. The original holograph manuscript of *The Time Machine* is preserved in the Wells Archive at the University of Illinois at Urbana-Champaign.

13. Wells, preface to *The Time Machine* (New York: Random House, 1931), ix.

7

Reception

"MY TRUMP CARD"

There can be no question that Wells had high hopes for the success of his first novel. Writing to his friend Elizabeth Healey when the story was about to be serialized in the *New Review* he told her:

> You may be interested to know that our ancient Chronic Argonauts of the *Science Schools Journal* has at last become a complete story and will appear as a serial in the *New Review*. . . . I'm praying it may go. It's my trump card and if it does not come off very much I shall know my place for the rest of my career.[1]

A few months later, on 14 May 1895, he was writing to the publisher William Heinemann urging publication of the book without delay, stressing that "the important thing to me is to get the book published." He concluded his letter, "Pardon my troubling you, but naturally I am in considerable suspense." Here we see the hopeful young author in an understandable state of anxiety concerning his first full-length work of fiction. The serialization had been well received, for in March 1895 an unsigned notice headed "A Man of Genius" appeared in the influential journal *Review of Reviews*. The review was written by the editor and critic W. T. Stead, a former editor of the *Pall Mall Gazette* and an important figure on the London literary scene. The notice ran as follows:

> H. G. Wells, who is writing the serial in the *New Review,* is a man of genius. His invention of the Time Machine was good, but his description of the ultimate evolution of society into the aristocrats and the capitalists who live on the surface of the earth in the sunshine, and the toilers who are doomed to live in the bowels of the earth in black darkness, in which they learn to see by the evolution of huge owl-like eyes, is gruesome and horrible to the last point. The story is not yet finished, but he has written enough to show that he has an imagination as gruesome as that of Poe.[2]

The significance of this review is threefold. First, it appeared well in advance of book publication of *The Time Machine,* after only the third monthly installment. It thus helped to stimulate interest in the *New Review* and to pave the way for an auspicious book launch. Second, it is convincing evidence that Wells was coming to the notice of leading editors and journalists (later the assistant editor of the *Review of Reviews*, Grant Richards, was to claim that he, not Stead, was the author of the unsigned notice—but he too was a leading journalist and a valuable contact for Wells to have made). Third, by declaring that Wells was a man of genius and comparing him with Poe the review brought him to the attention of a wider audience eager to read the work of a new writer.

It is important to understand that until 1894 his name was not widely known. The name H. G. Wells is so well known today in the English-speaking world and beyond that one has to make a real mental effort to contemplate a world in which the name was new. He was the author of elementary textbooks on biology and physiography published in 1893, but these had not sold widely. Beyond this his name would have been familiar to the readers of scholastic journals such as the *University Correspondent* and the *Educational Times,* both of which had published articles by him on educational topics, but virtually all his early fiction appeared anonymously or over a pseudonym. It was not until the summer of 1894 that his short stories began to be published over his own name, when a series of "Single Sitting Stories" appeared in the *Pall Mall Budget*. Unlike the *National Observer* articles, each installment in the *New Review* had been signed with the author's name. From now on the name H. G. Wells would be a name to be reckoned with. Buoyed up by this reception, he was anxious to see his work in print in a handsome book edition.

PUBLICATION

The Time Machine was published by Heinemann on 29 May 1895. It appeared simultaneously in hardback and paperback in an edition of ten thousand copies—a large print run for a hitherto little known author. Wells generously dedicated the book "To William Ernest Henley" and added a prefatory note:

> The substance of the first chapter of this story and of several paragraphs from the context appeared in the *National Observer* in 1894. The "Time Traveller's Story" appeared, almost as it stands here, in the pages of the *New Review*. The author desires to make the customary acknowledgements.

The circumstances of its publication suggest some indecision on the part of the publisher as to what kind of book it was. Its low price, two shillings and sixpence in cloth and one shilling and sixpence in wrappers (compared with the normal price of six shillings), suggests that Heinemann may have intended it to form one of a series of short literary works, economically priced—a popular genre at that time. Heinemann had its own series, the "Pioneer Library," including such titles as *The Green Carnation* by R. S. Hichens and *A Street in Suburbia* by E. W. Pugh; indeed, an advertisement for the series appears opposite the title page of the first edition of *The Time Machine*. While Heinemann made no assertion that the book formed part of this series, he evidently felt it would be attractive to buyers of popular fiction. Short, one-volume fiction was much in vogue in the 1890s. The demise of the three-decker novel coincided with the rise of the "shilling shocker": highly readable, melodramatic fiction marketed in paper covers and designed to be sold on railway-station book stalls. By packaging the book simultaneously in an elegant cloth format and in paperback Heinemann hoped to appeal to two markets at the same time: readers with a taste for the "literary novel" and the much larger audience seeking escapist romance. The large print run enabled the publisher to experiment with a variety of formats, as he continued to do over the following three years.

Wells was singularly fortunate in his timing, for the beginning of his literary career coincided with the decline and fall of the three-decker novel. This was the dominant form of fiction publishing from the 1820s until 1894—the practice of issuing novels in three volumes, each expensively priced. The system came to an abrupt end in 1894 when the two main lending libraries of the day, W. H. Smith's and Mudies, decided not to buy any work of fiction costing more than four shillings a volume. The three-decker was succeeded by the one-volume novel (normally costing six shillings), a practice that continued unchanged until well into the twentieth century. He was also fortunate in his choice of publisher, for William Heinemann was an enterprising man who, together with Chatto and Windus, played a leading role in the campaign to end the three-volume novel. Heinemann had enjoyed a huge success by issuing Hall Caine's *The Manxman* (1894) as a one-volume novel and published the work of other major writers including, R. L. Stevenson, Rudyard Kipling, and Israel Zangwill. The circumstances were therefore particularly favorable to the publication of a short first novel. The one-volume novel was very much in vogue, there was a demand for fiction of literary quality that could be read at a sitting; by issuing the book simultaneously in hardback and paperback Heinemann ensured that he reached the widest possible market.

EARLY REVIEWS

The Time Machine was not widely reviewed, but the notices it did receive were on the whole perceptive and favorable. An unsigned review in the *Daily Chronicle* drew a comparison between Wells and Stevenson:

> No two books could well be more unlike than *The Time Machine* and *The Strange Case of Dr Jekyll and Mr. Hyde*, but since the appearance of Stevenson's creepy romance we have had nothing in the domain of pure fantasy so bizarre as this "invention" by Mr. H. G. Wells. For his central idea Mr. Wells may be indebted to some previously published narrative suggestion, but if so we must confess ourselves entirely unacquainted with it, and so far as our knowledge goes he has produced in fiction that rarity that Solomon declared to be not merely rare but non-existent—a "new thing under the sun."[3]

The review goes on to praise the "Poe-like ingenuity of whimsical reasoning" in the opening chapter and continues: "The adventures of the Time Traveller among the Eloi and the Morlocks are conceived in the true spirit of fantasy—the effect of remoteness being achieved much more successfully than in such a book, for example, as Lord Lytton's *The Coming Race*." The review approves the literary quality of the novel, stating that the description of the dying world "grips the imagination as it is only gripped by genuinely imaginative work," and concludes—after some criticism of what it terms the "machinery" of the story—by asserting that the novel remains "a strikingly original performance."

Israel Zangwill, a popular novelist of the day, reviewed the book in the *Pall Mall Magazine*. While deeply skeptical of the notion of time-traveling, he was fulsome in his praise of the novel's literary qualities:

> Countless are the romances that deal with other times, other manners; endless have been the attempts to picture the time to come. Sometimes the future is grey with evolutionary perspectives, with previsions of a post-historic man, bald, toothless and fallen into his second infancy; sometimes it is gay with ingenuous foreglimpses of a renewed golden age of socialism and sentimentality. In his brilliant little romance *The Time Machine* Mr. Wells has inclined to the severer and more scientific form of prophecy—to the notion of a humanity degenerating inevitably from sheer pressure of physical comfort; but this not very novel conception, which was the theme of Mr. Besant's *Inner House*, and even partly of Pearson's *National Life and Character*, Mr. Wells has enriched by the invention of the Morlocks, a differentiated type of humanity that lives underground and preys upon the softer, prettier species that lives luxuriously in the sun, a fine imaginative creation worthy of Swift, and possibly not devoid of satirical reference to "the present discontents."[4]

These reviews are significant for several reasons. Both highlight the novel's literary and narrative power; the comparisons with Stevenson, Poe, and Swift must have been pleasing reading to a young man whose reputation hitherto rested on his short stories. Both highlight its fantastic and imaginative qualities. Above all, both, while drawing attention to some of the logical inconsistencies in the notion of time travel, are forced to concede the novel's very real merits. Zangwill is shrewd enough to observe that the story is "possibly not devoid of satirical references to the present discontents," thus focusing on the point that *The Time Machine* was not only a powerfully written fantasy of the future but also a satire bearing considerable relevance to the contemporary world. These notices, coming on top of Stead's enthusiastic report in the March *Review of Reviews*, ensured for *The Time Machine* a receptive audience. Indeed, it would not be too much to claim that it was *The Time Machine* that made Wells's literary reputation.

The "backlash" came in the form of a review in *The Spectator* by Richard Holt Hutton, an eminent editor and critic. After praising the book as "a very clever story," he rejects Wells's pessimistic vision of human evolution on religious and moral grounds, concluding:

> The nature of man must have altered not merely accidentally, but essentially, if the devotion to ease and amusement had left it sweet and serene. Matthew Arnold wrote in his unreal mood of agnosticism:—
>
> We, in some unknown Power's employ,
> Move on a rigorous line;
> Can neither, when we will, enjoy,
> Nor, when we will, resign.
>
> But it is not in some "unknown Power's employ" that we move on this "rigorous line." On the contrary, it is in the employ of a Power that has revealed itself in the Incarnation and the Cross. And we may expect with the utmost confidence that if the earth is still in existence in the year 802,701 A.D., either the A.D. will mean a great deal more than it means now, or else its inhabitants will be neither Eloi nor Morlocks. For in that case evil passions will by that time have led to the extinction of races spurred and pricked on by conscience and yet so frivolous or so malignant. Yet Mr. Wells's fanciful and lively dream is well worth reading, if only because it will draw attention to the great moral and religious factors in human nature that he appears to ignore.[5]

Hutton's review is perceptive in recognizing that *The Time Machine* is not only a scientific romance but also a salutary warning to contemporary society, but it castigates Wells for presenting a wholly secular view of evolution. Hutton's view seems to be that man is basically selfish and is too prone to evil passions to develop in the manner envisaged by Wells in his conception of the Eloi.

SCIENCE AND PROPHECY

An anonymous review in *Nature* praised the novel as "a clever piece of imagination" and drew attention to its scientific credentials:

> Ingeniously arguing that time may be regarded as the fourth dimension of which our faculties fail to give us any distinct impression, the author of this admirably-told story has conceived the idea of a machine that shall convey the traveller either backwards or forwards in time. Apart from its merits as a clever piece of

> imagination, the story is well worth the attention of the scientific reader, for the reason that it is based so far as possible on scientific data, and while not taking it too seriously, it helps one to get a connected idea of the possible results of the ever-continuing processes of evolution. Cosmical evolution, it may be remarked, is in some degree subject to mathematical investigations, and the author appears to be well acquainted with the results that have been obtained in this direction. It is naturally in the domain of social and organic evolution that the imagination finds its greatest scope.[6]

This review is important since it highlights the fact that *The Time Machine,* though a work of fiction, is based on scientific data. The reviewer recognizes that the novel is "admirably told" and that its author is acquainted with current ideas concerning evolution and the nature of time. By stressing that the novel "is well worth the attention of the scientific reader," the reviewer helped to ensure that *The Time Machine* received a wider readership than the normal fiction market. *Nature* was an influential journal, widely read in scientific and educational circles; a favorable notice within its pages was a significant bonus for Wells.

A notice in the *Saturday Review* focused on the novel's significance as a work of prophecy:

> It is a story that may not attain a popularity—one can prophesy nothing in these days of shoddy successes—but it is certainly a story of remarkable ability. Mr. Wells has been brave enough to essay a species of literature in which many others have failed, and his effort is a conspicuous success. Lord Lytton's *Coming Race* was a poor sort of invention, and nothing very much can be said in favor of *Erewhon. The Time Machine* is not in their category.[7]

We have to remind ourselves that *The Time Machine* was a first novel by a comparatively little-known author, yet already comparisons are being drawn with *The Coming Race* and *Erewhon,* to the detriment of these. It is almost certain that Wells read this notice, for he was a regular contributor to the *Saturday Review* from November 1894 onwards. Frank Harris had become the editor of the *Saturday Review* in September 1894 and had rapidly established it as one of the leading London journals, employing a brilliant team of writers including Max Beerbohm, Cunninghame Graham, Bernard Shaw, and Wells himself. Wells must have been gratified by the review, which concluded by praising his powers of description in the vision of the distant future. After quoting his picture of the desolate beach thirty million years hence, the reviewer concludes:

> The picture of this horrible desolation in the twilight of the world is magnificent, and barely represented by these detached fragments. We have quoted the extracts at some length as the only means of calling attention to a book of remarkable power and imagination, and to a writer of distinct and individual talent.

SCIENTIFIC PERSPECTIVE

An appraisal from a scientific perspective was offered by Wells's friend Richard Gregory, who had been a student with him at South Kensington. Gregory was one of the first critics to recognize Wells's significance as a writer to combine a scientific temperament with an imaginative vision, and to stress how firmly his dreams and speculations were rooted in the realities of science:

> Many writers of fiction have gathered material from the fairy-land of science, and have used it in the construction of literary fabrics, but none have done it more successfully than Mr. H. G. Wells. It is often easy to understand the cause of failure. The material may be used in such a way that there seems to be no connection between it and the background upon which it is seen: it may be so prominent that the threads with which it ought to harmonize are thrown into obscurity; or (and this is the worst of all) it may be employed by a writer whose knowledge of natural phenomena is not sufficient to justify his working with scientific colour. Mr. Wells makes none of these mistakes. Upon a groundwork of scientific fact, his vivid imagination and exceptional powers enable him to erect a structure that readers can find pleasure in contemplating.
>
> *The Time Machine*—considered by the majority of scientific readers to be Mr. Wells's best work—showed at once that a writer has arisen who was not only familiar with scientific facts, but also knew them intimately enough to present a view of the future.[8]

Gregory's central thesis is that Wells's romances are based upon "a groundwork of scientific fact" and that the vision of the future presented in *The Time Machine* has its origins in the biological conception of the human species he had imbibed as a science student under

Huxley. In stating that "many writers of fiction have gathered material from the fairy-land of science," Gregory could have named a host of writers, including, for example, Mary Shelley's *Frankenstein,* Edgar Allan Poe's *The Unparalleled Adventure of One Hans Pfaall* (a circumstantial account of a voyage to the moon by balloon), Bulwer Lytton's *The Coming Race,* or Jules Verne's *Twenty Thousand Leagues under the Sea.* The difference between these and Wells's romances, Gregory asserts, is that Wells's are extrapolations from known scientific facts and that his vision of human destiny, however fanciful it may seem, is firmly based on a Darwinian view of man.

CRITICAL TRENDS

We can now identify the main trends of criticism emerging in the years following publication of *The Time Machine.* There is, first, a recognition that Wells is an important and original writer of *fantasy*—that not since Poe has there been a writer of such vivid imaginative power. Critics were quick to seize on the novel's originality and the freshness of Wells's romance by comparison with the work of his predecessors.

Secondly, a number of critics drew attention to the satirical elements in the novel—that in the guise of a romance the author is presenting a critique of contemporary society. Zangwill's comparison with Swift is particularly apposite, a recognition that *The Time Machine* may on closer reading bear comparison with *Gulliver's Travels.* Thirdly, several commentators expressed skepticism of the whole notion of traveling through time, Zangwill boldly asserting "the absurdity of any attempt to grapple with the notion of Time," and the *Daily Chronicle* reviewer questioning why both the model and full-sized machines have disappeared from sight. Wells, he claims, constantly forgets that the Traveler is journeying through *time* and continually records effects suggesting travel through *space.* Finally, the *Spectator* review appraised the novel from an orthodox religious standpoint, dismissing it for its implicit rejection of the Christian scheme of salvation.

The critics were agreed on one point—that a new voice had arrived on the literary scene, and a voice of striking originality. Whatever their reservations as to the feasibility of time traveling or the probability of his conception of the future, all had to admit that Wells was a force to be reckoned with and that in his first novel he had said something genuinely *new.* While other writers had presented visions of the future—Bulwer Lytton, for example, in *The Coming Race* (1871) and W. H. Hudson in *A Crystal Age* (1887)—these did not possess the freshness and conviction of *The Time Machine*. Wells's novel had the force of a *myth* of compelling power.

On the whole, Wells had good reason to be satisfied with the novel's reception. Despite some reservations as to the pessimism of his central vision, the critics were unanimous in praising the novel for its literary and imaginative qualities, recognizing that Wells was an important new writer. The year 1895 was, indeed, Wells's *annus mirabilis*. In addition to *The Time Machine* three other books by him were published in that year: *Select Conversations with an Uncle, The Wonderful Visit,* and *The Stolen Bacillus and other Incidents* in June, September, and November, respectively. *The Time Machine* sold well and was widely discussed. The *Bookman* in its August issue featured an interview with Wells as a young writer of note. During that same year he drafted *The Island of Dr. Moreau* and commenced work on *The Wheels of Chance*. By the end of the year he had decided to abandon journalism altogether and concentrate all his energies on the writing of novels and short stories. He was no longer a journeyman living hand to mouth as a writer of articles and short stories; from now onward he was a novelist and author of scientific romances. He had "arrived" as a literary figure.

NOTES

1. Wells to Elizabeth Healey, 22 December 1894.
2. *Review of Reviews*, March 1895, 263, in Patrick Parrinder, ed., *H. G. Wells: The Critical Heritage* (London: Routledge, 1972), 33.
3. *Daily Chronicle,* 27 July 1895, 3.
4. *Pall Mall Magazine,* September 1895, 153–55.
5. *Spectator,* 13 July 1895, 41–43.
6. *Nature,* 18 July 1895, 268.
7. *Saturday Review,* 20 July 1895, 86–87.
8. *Nature,* 10 February 1898, 339–40.

Glossary

The Time Machine was originally published in 1895. During the century and more since then some of the words and phrases used by Wells have changed their meaning or become obscure. Other terms, such as "carters' whips" and "amateur cadger," will require explication for the modern reader.

Chapter	Page	
1	3	*recondite:* obscure, abstruse.
1	3	*trammels:* shackles. Wells is using the term loosely.
1	5	*Simon Newcomb:* Newcomb (1835–1909) was president of the American Mathematical Society and editor of the *American Journal of Mathematics.*
1	6	*Gravitation limits us there:* Wells is writing in 1894. The airplane was not invented until 1903, and commercial aviation did not become practicable until the 1920s.
1	7	*Little-go:* a preliminary examination at Oxford and Cambridge Universities.
1	8	*Burslem:* an industrial town in the Staffordshire Potteries. Wells knew the area, as he had stayed there in 1888 while convalescing after an illness. Parts of *In the Days of the Comet* (1906) and *The New Machiavelli* (1911) are set in Burslem.
2	12	*Linnaean:* A learned society named in honor of the Swedish botanist Linnaeus.

2 15 *Amateur Cadger:* pretending to be a beggar.

2 15 *eke out his modest income with a crossing:* In Victorian London, sweepers were employed to keep road crossings free of horse manure. (See also the following entry.)

2 15 *Nebuchadnezzar phases:* The reference is to the Babylonian King Nebuchadnezzar, who lost his kingdom and was transformed into a beast (Daniel 4: 4–28). The Editor feels this would account for the Traveller's untidy appearance.

2 16 *Rosebery:* Earl Rosebery (1847–1929) was prime minister in 1894. The reference here is not to Rosebery himself but to a racehorse owned by him.

2 16 *Hettie Potter*. The origin of this reference is not known. The most likely explanation is that she was a music-hall star of the time.

3 18 *Mrs Watchett:* The Time Traveler's housekeeper.

3 23 *buskin:* a thick-soled boot.

4 24 *Dresden-china:* fine decorated china noted for its fragility.

4 30 *wells still existing:* This is a pun on Wells's own name. Wells is speculating whether his writings will still be known in the world of the distant future. (See also his comment on page 68 on the futility of literary ambition.)

5 39 *Occidental:* Western, characteristic of the Western world.

5 41 *sepulture:* burial.

5 45 *a queer notion of Grant Allen's:* the reference is to "Pallinghurst Barrow," a short story by Grant Allen (1848–99), a novelist and thinker who deeply influenced Wells.

5 45 *Three several times:* this is not a misprint. Wells is using the word "several" in the sense of "separate"—that is, he sees the Morlocks on three separate occasions.

5 47 *Lemur:* a primitive mammal.

5 50 *cicerone:* a guide. In many nineteenth century utopias the narrator meets a "convenient cicerone" who proceeds to explain the basis of the future society. See, for example, Edward Bellamy's *Looking Backward* (1888) and William Morris's *News from Nowhere* (1891).

6	52	*Combe Wood:* An area of Surrey midway between Richmond and Banstead.
6	52	*Banstead:* A village in Surrey, close to Epsom Downs. Wells knew the area, as he lived at nearby Sutton during 1893.
6	52	*Palace of Green Porcelain:* Wells may have had in mind such a building as Alexandra Palace, London, constructed in 1873 and a prominent landmark on the crest of a hill.
6	54	*a vast arched cavern:* The image of a dimly lit cavern partially illuminated by a match is also used by Wells in his seminal essay "The Rediscovery of the Unique" (1891).
6	55	*halitus:* a vapor.
7	58	*Carlovignan kings:* Three ninth-century kings noted for their degeneracy. The correct spelling is "Carlovingian."
7	61	*precessional cycle:* the rotation of the pole of the earth's equator round the pole of the ecliptic. The rotation is slightly unequal, as the earth is not a perfect sphere. The complete cycle takes roughly twenty-five thousand years.
7	63	*Carlyle-like scorn:* As a student Wells had read much Thomas Carlyle (1795–1881). In his *Past and Present* (1843) Carlyle predicted the demise of the aristocracy.
8	65	*South Kensington:* The reference is not to the College where Wells had been a student but to the South Kensington Museum, a group of science and art museums on Exhibition Road, London.
8	67	*the "area" of a London house:* a narrow enclosed yard below street level.
8	68	*tail-coat:* a man's formal coat, with narrow tails at the back.
8	69	*steatite monster:* carved from soapstone.
9	73	*as it spit*. Most editions of *The Time Machine* render this passage "as it split," which clearly makes no sense. The original manuscript has "as it spat" or "as it spit" (the handwriting is unclear).
11	81	*the work of the tidal drag was done:* A widely held theory in Victorian times was that the universe would gradually slow down. According to this

		theory the movement of the planets round the sun would slowly reduce in speed, so that the length of the day on earth would gradually increase.
11	82	*carters' whips:* A carter was the driver of a horse drawn vehicle designed to carry heavy loads. The driver used a whip to control his horse.
12	86	*Hillyer:* note that Hillyer is the narrator of the outer narrative or "frame" of *The Time Machine*—that is, he is the narrator of chapters 1, 2, and the epilogue.
12	86	*Pall Mall Gazette:* a popular London daily newspaper. The *Gazette* published much of Wells's early journalism.
12	88	*gynaeceum:* the reproductive organ of a flower.
Epilogue	91	*Cretaceous:* belonging to the uppermost system of Mesozoic rocks, 140–65 million years ago.
Epilogue	91	*saurians:* a fossil reptile resembling a lizard.
Epilogue	91	*Jurassic:* the middle division of the Mesozoic rocks, 195–140 million years ago.
Epilogue	91	*plesiosaurus:* a marine reptile with a long neck and four flippers.
Epilogue	91	*Oolitic:* characteristic of the Jurassic geological period.
Epilogue	91	*saline:* salty.
Epilogue	91	*Triassic:* The oldest of the Mesozoic rocks, 230–195 million years ago.

Bibliographical Essay

> There is, he believes, in the ultimate reckoning something said in these volumes that was not said before, and something shaped that was not shaped before.
>
> —H. G. Wells, introduction to the Atlantic Edition of his works, 1924

> Now, instead of reversing the levers I had pulled them over so as to go forward with them, and when I came to look at these indicators I found that the thousands hand was sweeping round as fast as the seconds hand of a watch—into futurity.
>
> —H. G. Wells, *The Time Machine*, 1895

THE TIME MACHINE AND THE TWENTIETH CENTURY

During the opening years of the twentieth century, *The Time Machine* was frequently reprinted in response to popular demand. It was translated into many foreign languages and continued to sell widely in English and American editions in addition to the popular paperback edition issued by Tauchnitz.

It was not until 1915 that the first full-length critical study of Wells's work was published, written by the English novelist J. D. Beresford. In a study simply entitled *H. G. Wells,* Beresford reviewed the whole range of Wells's writings published up to that date, observing that in his view Wells's principal achievement "is that he has set up the ideal of a finer civilization, of a more generous life than that in which we live; an ideal that, if it is still too high for us of this generation, will be appreciated and followed by the people of the future." His appraisal of *The Time Machine* is interesting and perceptive:

> The prophecy is less convincing than the wonderful sight of the declining earth some million years later, sinking slowly into the dying fires of the worn-out sun. Man and the vertebrates have disappeared, and the highest wonder of animal life is represented by giant crustaceans, which in turn give way to a lower form. We have a vision of an involution that shall succeed the highest curve of development; of life ending where it began in the depths of the sea, as the initial energy of the solar system is dissipated and the material of it returns to rest at the temperature of the absolute zero. And the picture is made more horrible to the imaginative by the wonder whether the summit of the evolutionary curve has not already been reached—or it may be passed in the days of the Greek philosophers.
>
> *The Time Machine,* despite certain obvious faults of imagination and style, is a brilliant fantasy; and it affords a valuable picture of the young Wells looking at the world, with his normal eyes, and finding it, more particularly, incomplete. At the age of twenty-seven or so, he has freed himself very completely from the bonds of conventional thought, and is prepared to examine, and to present life from the detached standpoint of one who views it all from a respectable distance; but who is able, nevertheless—an essential qualification—to enter life with all the passion and generosity of his own humanity.[1]

These comments, written twenty years after the original publication of the novel, reveal Beresford's grasp of its enduring significance—first, as an inversion of the widely held notion that evolution must inevitably lead to progress; and second, as a striking demonstration of Wells's power of detachment. In drawing attention to *The Time Machine* as "a vision of an involution that shall succeed the highest curve of development" and posing the question "whether the summit of the evolutionary curve has not already been reached," Beresford highlighted what is arguably *The Time Machine*'s most important and original contribution to modern thought—its implicit rejection of the idea of progress and its challenge to the notion that each stage of the evolutionary process must necessarily lead to advancement. Beresford grasps that Wells's vision "of life ending where it began in the depths of the sea" gives a cyclical form to his conception of human destiny and compels the reader to face the implications of a world in which

Homo sapiens has disappeared. Most perceptive of all is his observation that Wells presents life "from the detached standpoint of one who views it all from a respectable distance" but who is able nevertheless to enter life with passion. Wells's extraordinary ability to detach himself from everyday concerns (as his narrator expresses it in *The War of the Worlds*: "At times I suffer from the strangest sense of detachment from myself and the world about me; I seem to watch it all from the outside, from somewhere inconceivably remote, out of time, out of space, out of the stress and tragedy of it all")[2] is one of the most memorable aspects of *The Time Machine*, particularly of chapter 11, with its haunting image of a dying planet and a blood-red sun. At the same time, Beresford notes, Wells enters life "with all the passion and generosity of his own humanity." The Time Traveler is at once the skeptical man of science and the romantic determined to challenge his apparently inevitable fate.

In the same year as Beresford's study, the American scholar Van Wyck Brooks, in *The World of H. G. Wells,* argued that there was nothing fundamentally unsound with Wells's exposition of time traveling, though the idea of time as the fourth dimension had been challenged by the philosopher W. B. Pitkin.[3] In his essay "Time and Pure Activity" Pitkin asserted that the underlying concept of *The Time Machine* was scientifically impossible, a view advanced twenty years earlier by Israel Zangwill in the review noted earlier.[4] The significance of these critical studies is their implicit assertion that Wells was a major writer, meriting detailed scrutiny. Beresford, by demonstrating the literary and imaginative qualities of his work, and Brooks, by underlining the skeptical basis of his thought, invited readers to study Wells with serious attention as a major novelist and thinker. The time had clearly come for a reappraisal of Wells and an assessment of his contribution to the world of letters. The First World War, with its immense dislocation of civilization, rendered any such reassessment inopportune, but with the coming of peace and the return to normality publishers on both sides of the Atlantic began considering the idea of a collected edition.

THE ATLANTIC EDITION

During 1924, Fisher Unwin in London and Charles Scribners in New York issued a uniform edition of Wells's works in twenty-eight volumes, the text throughout having been read and revised by the author. Each volume of this collection, the Atlantic Edition, contained a specially written introduction by Wells. In his introduction to volume 1, containing *The Time Machine, The Wonderful Visit,* and eleven short stories, Wells acknowledges that he could "no more touch it or change it than if it were the work of an entirely different person." Looking at the book again thirty years after it was written, he confesses he finds it "hard and "clever" and youthful." After a gap of so many years he could not bring himself to alter the text (apart from one or two very minor stylistic amendments)[5] but confined himself to a drastic renumbering of the chapters—reducing the number of chapters from sixteen to twelve—and removing the chapter titles. He evidently felt that in the original arrangement some of the sections were of insufficient length and that in artistic terms the narrative would gain from a reduction in the number of divisions. The deletion of the chapter headings is perhaps less easy to justify, but Wells evidently convinced himself that this was an improvement.

The question of what the status of the Atlantic Edition is, or should be, has not been satisfactorily resolved. Clearly it represents an authoritative text, in the sense that each volume was revised by the author and carries a preface describing the genesis of the novel and the author's current views upon it. However Wells does not seem to have taken any action to suppress or withdraw the original texts, many of which have continued to be reprinted in a variety of popular editions. The result is that in the case of each of his popular novels and romances, the texts of the first edition and the Atlantic Edition continue to circulate side by side. From the point of view of Wells scholarship this is an unsatisfactory situation. What was needed was a scholarly, reliable, annotated edition of all the standard works—but it was not until seventy years later that the first variorum edition of a Wells novel appeared.[6]

WELLS AND TIME

Wells continued to be fascinated by the idea of time travel and the notion of communication between four dimensional universes. In his novel *Men Like Gods* (1923), a representative group of travelers find themselves transposed by means of a "kink in space" to a world thousands of years hence. *The Dream* (1924) posits the reverse situation, in which a citizen of two thousand years hence imagines himself transposed to the twentieth century. The publication of J. W. Dunne's *An Experiment with Time* (1927) stimulated him immensely. Dunne's notion of "serial time" and the theory that precognition may be possible through a systematic analysis of dreams exercised his imagination. He toyed with Dunne's ideas for some years and speculated about them in an article, "New Light on Mental Life," and in a short story, "The

Queer Story of Brownlow's Newspaper."[7] In the latter, set in the year 1931, a man reads a newspaper from the year 1971 offering tantalizing glimpses of the future. Wells continued to allow his imagination to play with the idea and in *The Shape of Things to Come* (1933) elaborated a full-scale "history of the future" from 1930 to the year 2106. The book purports to be the "dream book" of a Dr Philip Raven; in an intriguing introduction Wells explains that the ostensible narrator has "seen" the narrative in a series of vivid dreams—an idea he had previously employed in his short story "A Dream of Armageddon," published in 1901. It is apparent from "The Queer Story of Brownlow's Newspaper" and *The Shape of Things to Come* that throughout his life Wells was intrigued by the idea of dislocations in time and continued to speculate on what would happen if one were to be transported abruptly to a world with a different timescale from our own.

In 1931 he was invited by the leading New York publisher Random House to write a special preface for a new edition of *The Time Machine*. The edition was to be handsomely printed and bound, and would include designs by the artist W. A. Dwiggins. Wells responded with a carefully written preface reviewing the circumstances in which *The Time Machine* had been written and summarizing his present attitude to his first published novel. The preface is of considerable interest as an indication of his attitude to his early work. Intellectually, it is clear that his attitude is one of critical detachment—"it is obviously the work of an inexperienced writer"; it is in his view "a very unequal book"; it is "a slender story," "a very undergraduate performance." Emotionally, it is equally clear that he regards the book with warm affection. Indeed, he continues, "he hugs his vanity very pleasantly at times when his dear old *Time Machine* crops up once more in essays and speeches." But the key passage in his introduction is the reference to Swift: "In his adolescence Swift had exercised a tremendous fascination upon him and the naïve pessimism of this picture of the human future is, like the kindred *Island of Doctor Moreau,* a clumsy tribute to a master to whom he owes an enormous debt."

The word "naïve" in this sentence suggests that Wells had departed from the pessimism of his early work and was now embracing a more sanguine vision of the future. His son Anthony West, always a perceptive commentator on his father's writings, has observed that "Wells's 'progressive' writing represents an attempt to straddle irreconcilable positions, and it involved a perpetual conflict of a wasteful character." West continues: "In all too much of his work he is engaged in shouting down his own better judgment."[8] It is true that during the final decades of his life Wells was writing such apparently optimistic books as *The Work, Wealth and Happiness of Mankind* (1932), *The Shape of Things to Come* (1933), and *Star Begotten* (1937). But he was also writing deeply pessimistic stories, such as *Mr Blettsworthy on Rampole Island* (1928), *The Croquet Player* (1936), and *You Can't Be Too Careful* (1941), works that hold out little if any hope for mankind and are imbued with sombre Swiftian skepticism. The fact is that over an extremely prolific literary career spanning fifty years his moods inevitably fluctuated between optimism and pessimism. His use of the word "naïve" with reference to the pessimism of *The Time Machine* should therefore be treated with caution. Fundamentally, he did not depart from the sombre realism of his first novel—above all else Wells was a realist and knew that ultimately man is an animal subject to the normal laws of evolution. In this context it is appropriate that the preface acknowledges the importance of Swift as "a master to whom he owes an enormous debt." His indebtedness to Swift was profound and enduring.

In anticipation of his eightieth birthday on 21 September 1946, Penguin Books published a commemorative edition of ten of his works: *Tono-Bungay, The New Machiavelli, The War of the Worlds, A Short History of the World, The Time Machine, The Island of Doctor Moreau, The History of Mr Polly, Love and Mr Lewisham, The Invisible Man,* and *Kipps*. One hundred thousand copies of each volume were printed. It was a tribute that meant much to him, for he cared far more for his posthumous reputation than he publicly acknowledged. But he did not live to see his birthday. Five weeks before, on 13 August 1946, he died peacefully in his sleep.

The funeral service was attended by a distinguished gathering of friends and relatives. In his address J. B. Priestley paid tribute to Wells's achievement:

> His literary genius was rich and rare—the best of his novels and short stories are among the finest creations of our time—but he belongs not only to English Literature, but also to world history, as a great educator and as the chief prophet of this age of transition, long foreshadowing, with pity and passion, the shape of things to come.[9]

WELLS IN MID-CENTURY

By 1950 Wells's critical reputation was at a low ebb. His death had been followed by a reaction against his work, a reaction confirmed by Vincent Brome's biography—the first full-length appraisal of his life—published in 1951. Brome's lively but unbalanced study tended to confirm the popular image of Wells as an author whose best work had all been written by 1920. Though Brome's biography is highly readable, it suffers from being based almost entirely on secondary sources, and it lacks the scholarship that was to come in later biographies. The materials necessary to write a full-scale scholarly study of his life and work were simply not available at that time.

In 1950 Norman Nicholson published a stimulating study of Wells's literary achievement, singling out *The Time Machine* as "quite unmistakable Wells." After describing the nightmare world of the Morlocks Nicholson continued:

> The story of *The Time Machine* is rather cold, however, because it was not possible to transmit more than one person of our own age into the future, and the attractive, adolescent Weena does not compensate for the lack of humanity. It is indeed in a purely non-human vision that the book reaches its finest passages. The Traveler escapes from the Morlocks by means of the Time Machine and travels into the remote future, when both the earth and the sun are cooling and our solar system is in decline. Here Wells succeeded in placing before the reader a vision of the world in cosmic time. The theory of evolution was widely known by the end of the nineteenth century and man's conception of history had broadened from that of a few score centuries to that of great geological ages. But even this view had its peak and pivot in Man. Wells now revealed a vision of time in which Man is merely part of a curve. For one whose outlook was as humanist as his it was an act of humility, and the picture of this lethargic dying world is among the most significant passages in the popular literature of the last sixty years.[10]

Nicholson's appraisal of *The Time Machine* is not wholly favorable, for he criticizes it for its immaturity and lack of assurance. His insistence that it is "in a purely non-human vision that the book reaches its finest passages" would probably find wide assent, as would his assertion that one of the most striking aspects of the novel is its vision of time "in which man is merely part of a curve." His description of the vision of the world thirty million years hence as being "among the most significant passages in the popular literature of the last sixty years" (i.e., 1890–1950) would have probably seemed an extravagant claim at the time but would find a more ready acceptance today.

BERGONZI'S *THE EARLY H. G. WELLS*

After the death of any major novelist there is inevitably a period in which his or her work is digested. One stands back, as it were, and seeks to assess the writer's significance and to separate the wheat from the chaff. In Wells's case the process was a slow one; it was not until fifteen years after his death that it was possible to view him dispassionately and assess his permanent contribution to English literature. One of the first serious appraisals of his work was Bernard Bergonzi's study *The Early H. G. Wells* (1961), a survey and critique of the scientific romances. In a careful analysis of Wells's use of imagery and symbolism in *The Time Machine,* Bergonzi notes the way in which "its central narrative is polarised between opposed groups of imagery, the paradisal and the demonic, representing extreme forms of human desire and repulsion." He sees *The Time Machine* as a romance and not as a piece of realistic fiction, noting therefore that "it conveys its meaning in poetic fashion through images, not by the revelation of character in action." He insists that the novel is a work possessing considerable literary and imaginative power and that "despite the complexity of its thematic elements, Wells's art is such that the story is a skilfully wrought imaginative whole, a single image."[11]

Bergonzi's achievement in *The Early H. G. Wells* was to submit the scientific romances to sustained critical examination, and in doing so to demonstrate that they are legitimate subjects for detailed academic scrutiny. Prior to his study Wells's fiction had received comparatively little critical attention; indeed, the prevailing attitude to his work in the immediate aftermath of his death was one of disparagement.[12] It has to be said that Wells was paying the price for having written too much and too unevenly; in view of the sheer volume of his work and its bewildering range, it is hardly surprising that there was a reaction against it. Bergonzi helped to redress this balance by subjecting his early work to a thoughtful, sober analysis, paying careful attention to its thematic and allegorical elements. In doing so he rendered a signal service to Wells scholarship and paved the way for a new generation of critics eager to explore Wells's significance to literary history.

THE TIME MACHINE REASSESSED

In his important essay "The Logic of "Prophecy" in *The Time Machine,"* Robert M. Philmus poses the question: why did the Traveler feel a compulsion to resume his time traveling? In attempting to answer this question Philmus argues that the narrative conforms to an inner logic that determines its outcome:

> That the structure of *The Time Machine* encompasses, and thereby defines the limits of, the Traveller's point of view indicates that the romance follows an inner logic of its own, a logic, like that governing the Time Traveller's vision, which compels ultimate consequences from a given premise. Accordingly, the logic that necessitates the Traveller's vanishing into the world of his vision derives from how he accepts that vision. His insistence that "The story I told you was true" suggests that he takes his vision literally, that he allows it the same ontological status that he himself has. Hence to dramatize the assertion that he has told the literal truth, he must go back into the Fourth Dimension: since he cannot accept the "prophecy" as metaphor, he must disappear into the dimension where it "exists." The demand that his vision be literally true, in other words, requires the Traveller to be no more real than it is; and his return into the Fourth Dimension fulfils this demand.[13]

The point is surely a valid one: the fact that the Traveler (in common with the miniature time machine) has disappeared enhances the veracity of the story. By returning to the fourth dimension the Traveler has demonstrated the truthfulness of his vision and vindicated himself before a largely skeptical audience.

In a significant essay entitled "A Grammar of Form and a Criticism of Fact: *The Time Machine* as a Structural Model for Science Fiction" (1973),[14] the American Wells scholar Darko Suvin proceeds on the hypothesis that "the basic device of *The Time Machine* is an opposition of the Time Traveller's visions of the future to the ideal reader's norm of complacent bourgeois class consciousness with its belief in linear progress, Spencerian 'Social Darwinism,' and the like." In a carefully written argument Suvin demonstrates Wells's indebtedness to Huxley, especially the latter's essay *Evolution and Ethics*. Suvin elaborates the theme of biological regression that underpins *The Time Machine* and contrasts Darwin's evolutionary vision with that evinced in Wells's novel. Through a methodical analysis of the novel's narrative structure, Suvin argues that *The Time Machine* presents an exponentially regressing rhythm that logically culminates in the extinction of man—the logic of the story "makes it imperative that the Traveller finally vanish: its final and validating member can only be zero or nonexistence, extinction." Suvin's essay has exercised an important influence on students of *The Time Machine*. Through its detailed analysis of the narrative and its extrapolation of the pattern of opposites upon which it is based—light and darkness, life and death, tamed and untamed, evolutive and devolutive—he demonstrates convincingly the internal symmetry on which the novel is based. Moreover he draws attention to its allegorical significance as a dramatization of the age old confrontation between Everyman and Death—a confrontation that has served as a model for both ancient fable and modern science fiction.

The Time Traveller: The Life of H. G. Wells, by Norman and Jeanne Mackenzie, published in 1973, was the first full-scale biography of Wells to appear. In a sympathetic appraisal of *The Time Machine* the Mackenzies noted that "a sense of time, as the dimension against which man's past and future might be measured, and his present complacency judged, was the most original contribution that Wells brought to English fiction." They continued: "His feeling for the span of time was both biological and cosmic":

> The contrast between a smug faith in inevitable progress and the possibilities of degeneration was the main point that Wells was making when he launched his Time Traveler out of a cosy Richmond dinner-party into a series of increasingly frightening situations. . . . By setting the end of *The Time Machine* so far in the future, beyond the Golden Age in which the Time Traveller enters the world of the charming but decadent Eloi, beyond even the Sunset of Mankind, Wells converted Huxley's cosmic pessimism into a vision of the final nullity beyond all temporal ideas of good and evil.[15]

The Mackenzies conclude that *The Time Machine* is a deeply pessimistic work, for "to the question, Is it Dawn or Dusk? Wells had answered that mankind was ultimately doomed, and that its prospect is not Salvation but Extinction." The biography is illuminated throughout by penetrating insight and lively scholarship. By subjecting the whole range of Wells's life and thought to detailed scrutiny, the Mackenzies stimulated widespread discussion of his works and persuaded readers in both Britain and the United States to return to his novels afresh. Within this renewed attention to Wells *The Time Machine* inevitably received a resurgence of interest.

In their excellent anthology *H. G. Wells: Early Writings in Science and Science Fiction*, published in 1975, Robert M. Philmus and another distinguished American scholar, David Y. Hughes, presented a compilation of hitherto uncollected writings of Wells, including the complete text of the *National Observer Time Machine* and a range of early essays on scientific and related themes. In their preface Philmus and Hughes explained that "the primary purpose of this anthology is to make available in one volume a selection of H. G. Wells's hitherto unreprinted writings of the 1880s and 1890s relating to science and the sciences." By bringing together this material in a carefully edited text with critical introductions and apparatus, Philmus and Hughes demonstrated the continuing relevance of Wells's thought and the integrity of his scientific vision. By drawing attention to his pessimism they helped to counterbalance the widely held misconception that Wells was an apostle of technological progress per se. The inclusion of such essays as "Zoological Retrogression," "On Extinction," and "Human Evolution: An Artificial Process" served as a salutary reminder that the stoical realism of *The Time Machine* was integral to his thought and was grounded in the biological vision he had imbibed from his mentor T. H. Huxley.

In their introduction Philmus and Hughes question the widely held view that the bulk of Wells's early writings are ephemeral. "Many of them . . . have some intrinsic worth as literature. In that offhand, colloquial style of which he is a master, Wells speculates on the nature and destiny of man." Grouping the material under rubrics rather than in chronological order serves to clarify Wells's ideas and to demonstrate the significance of his early scientific essays in understanding *The Time Machine* and *The Island of Doctor Moreau*.

Wells's own judgment that much of his early journalism "was good enough to print but not worth reprinting"[16] had been taken too readily at face value and had led to a neglect of the early writings (with the notable exception of Bergonzi, noted above). "For Wells, as for his contemporaries," Philmus and Hughes observe, "the center of biological thinking had become the theory of evolution. That theory entailed, among other consequences, a radical reorientation of conceptions of space and time."[17] *Early Writings in Science and Science Fiction* marks a watershed in Wells studies. It presents in an attractive format the fruits of scholarly research and, in focusing on the scientific aspects of Wells's work, complements the literary and artistic approach exemplified by Bergonzi. The anthology stimulated renewed attention to the early writings, including the scientific essays and short stories, and set an extremely high standard for later scholars to follow.

In a perceptive essay, "The Time Machine: H. G. Wells's Journey through Death" (1981), Patrick Parrinder puts forward the persuasive hypothesis that "Wells made himself into a creative writer by looking into his own imminent death and projecting his imagination beyond that death."[18] Recalling that Wells had been very seriously ill before embarking on *The Chronic Argonauts,* Parrinder asserted that "we may see *The Time Machine* not only as one of the most remarkable, but as in a sense the most heroic of his books." He continues that "*The Time*

Machine survives first and foremost as an unrivalled extrapolation of the Darwinian vision of man," and he reiterates Wells's assertion—implicit in the novel—that "the coming death of humanity cannot affect our actions in the here and now." The stoical realism of *The Time Machine* and *The Island of Doctor Moreau,* Parrinder argues, constitutes Wells's most enduring legacy. By triumphing over a nearly fatal illness at the age of twenty-one Wells cheated death, surviving to become one of the leading writers of his day. By outwitting the Morlocks and observing dispassionately the future of the human race, the Time Traveler escaped his apparently inevitable fate and triumphed over his destiny. Thus Parrinder invites us to see the novel not simply as Wells's literary apprenticeship but as an apprenticeship deeply personal to its author. The novel is a vindication of the human spirit and of man's determination to triumph over obstacles, whatever the cost.

THE LOGIC OF FANTASY

The reassessment of the novel is continued in several important works published in the 1980s. In *The Logic of Fantasy: H. G. Wells and Science Fiction,* John Huntington identifies *The Time Machine* as a work based on a dynamic of opposites:

> Wells's use of balanced opposition and symbolic mediation as a way of thinking finds its most perfect form in *The Time Machine.* If the novella imagines a future, it does so not as a forecast but as a way of contemplating the structures of our present civilization. At one level *The Time Machine* presents a direct warning about the disastrous potential of class division. But at a deeper level it investigates large questions of difference and domination, and rather than settling the issues, it constructs unresolvable conflicts that return us to the central dilemmas that have characterized the evolutionary debate we looked at in the first chapter.[19]

In a perceptive essay Huntington focuses on this pattern of opposing concepts: pessimism and optimism, Eloi and Morlocks, progress and regression, change and stasis, human and beast. In the contrast and interplay between these differing concepts, Huntington argues, lies much of the tension implicit in the narrative. These tensions and ambiguities, he asserts, are left unresolved. The essay concludes by comparing the original story with the George Pal film version, made in 1960, stressing that Pal "avoids facing the very conflicts that define Wells's work." Because the film version removes the contradictions inherent in the narrative, it is greatly inferior to the novel.

In a critical study of Wells published in 1985, the British scholar John Batchelor argues that three of his scientific romances "stand out as indisputably permanent and major": *The Time Machine, The Island of Doctor Moreau,* and *The War of the Worlds.* Batchelor is one of the first commentators to acknowledge the central importance of Weena:

> It is important that the Traveller's sardonic detachment from the Eloi and Morlocks in the early version is replaced in the finished story by the confused feelings bred in him by Weena; indeed, I would argue that the introduction of Weena effects the change from a succession of coldly brilliant ideas to a persuasive and complex work of fiction. She is a moral touchstone whose presence rebukes the Traveller for his attempt to take refuge from his own distress at the fate that has overtaken mankind.[20]

Because Weena arouses feelings of affection, sympathy, and attraction, Batchelor argues, she transforms what would otherwise be a dry intellectual exercise into a narrative that engages the reader's emotions, wringing from the Traveler the admission that "the Eloi had kept too much of the human form not to claim my sympathy." Batchelor points out that *The Time Machine* combines a confidence in the validity of human achievement and scientific enquiry with a fear of the unknown: "The Traveller is fundamentally pessimistic about the future of man but has a continuing drive to *know* which sends him on his last (and presumably fatal) journey." This antithesis between skepticism and curiosity provides the narrative with a tension that energizes Wells's text.

THE WRITING OF *THE TIME MACHINE*

In 1984 the French scholar Bernard Loing published *H. G. Wells a L'oeuvre: Les débuts d'un écrivain,* a detailed study of the composition of three early Wells texts: *The Time Machine, The Island of Doctor Moreau,* and *Love and Mr. Lewisham.*[21] Better known under its English title *H. G. Wells at Work,* Loing's study is an essential contribution to Wellsian scholarship. The book contains a comprehensive account of the writing of *The Time Machine,* including a detailed chronology of its composition, an examination of the various drafts and versions, and textual analysis. An appendix reproduces sample pages from the holograph manuscript, together with relevant correspondence between Wells and his literary circle during the years of composition.

H. G. Wells at Work marks a significant milestone in Wells studies, because in it for the first time Wells's methods of work are subjected to careful academic scrutiny. Loing demonstrates that the novel was composed with elaborate care and passed through a complex process of revision extending over several years. In doing so Loing vindicates Wells against the accusation that he was a careless writer who did not take pains over his work; he helped to pave the way for later critical studies from such writers as Philmus, Hughes, and Harry Geduld.[22]

In a critical study of Wells's fiction published in 1987, Michael Draper ably summarizes the novel's principal themes, reminding his readers that "into this, his first book-length story, Wells poured ideas and obsessions he had nursed for years, working over the text again and again till it rang true." He goes on to draw attention to "the playful quality of all Wells's earlier fiction, which makes its primary appeal as entertainment and resists over-literal interpretation. . . . Analysed by critics, *The Time Machine* may be, as some have called it, desolating; simply read, however, it is enormous fun."[23]

Draper is surely right to remind us of the merits of *The Time Machine* as a sheer piece of storytelling. As a vivid, page-turning narrative the story has few equals in our time. The reader becomes totally absorbed in the Traveler's adventures, beguiled by Wells's skill in drawing us into his fantasy.

THE DEFINITIVE TIME MACHINE

The Definitive Time Machine, edited by Harry M. Geduld (1987), brings together in one volume the Atlantic Edition text of 1924 and the texts of earlier versions, including *The Chronic Argonauts* and the *National Observer Time Machine*, along with a range of supplementary material. The most valuable feature of Geduld's work is its excellent critical introduction, reviewing the novel's structure and background, and his detailed annotations of the text—these will be of permanent relevance to scholars and students. Geduld states that "like *Alice in Wonderland* and *Gulliver's Travels*, *The Time Machine* embodies many levels of meaning and appeals to readers of virtually every age. . . . It was also the first significant dystopia and one of the earliest visions of man's ultimate destiny to be based on serious scientific speculation."[24] He argues that the novel had its genesis in Wells's childhood experiences including his reading, his religious upbringing, and certain juvenile fears and fantasies. For example, the nightmare qualities of the Morlocks may have had their origin in Wells's childhood fear of gorillas—engendered by a fearsome illustration in Wood's *Illustrated Natural History*—and in his fascination with "forbidden" subjects, such as hell and damnation. His childhood reading, including the Bible and

Pilgrim's Progress, may have influenced the religious imagery and narrative technique employed in the novel, particularly the sense of the Time Traveler as a lone protagonist journeying through a strange land.

Despite its title, however, *The Definitive Time Machine* cannot claim to be a fully definitive work, since it does not present a variorum text. We still await a variorum edition of *The Time Machine,* a reliable text together with all the known variant readings; this will surely come. In the meantime Geduld's work succeeds admirably in its own terms as a critical edition bringing together in an accessible format a useful selection of expository material.

To summarize, then, it is possible to identify the main lines of criticism of *The Time Machine* that have emerged since Wells's death in 1946:

- A study of the imagery and symbolism employed in the text, with particular reference to the use of opposed groups of imagery—for instance, paradisal and demonic
- The narrative as a text conforming to an internal logic that necessitates the Traveler's return to the fourth dimension
- The narrative as a paradigm of biological regression, challenging the reader's assumption of linear progress and replacing this with the concept of human extinction
- The narrative as a heroic text in the sense that it projects Wells's imagination beyond his own death
- The narrative as a fable that presents in the form of a metaphor the drama of man pitting his intelligence against his adversaries
- The narrative as an autobiographical text having its roots embedded in Wells's psyche, in particular his religious upbringing and childhood fears.

TWO CRITICAL EDITIONS

A century after the original publication of *The Time Machine* in 1895, two critical editions of the text were published, both of them of value to students. The World's Classics edition of the novel, edited by Patrick Parrinder, was published by Oxford University Press, New York, in 1996. This incorporates the text of the novel as revised by Wells for the Atlantic Edition of 1924, together with full critical apparatus, including a select bibliography, a note on the various texts of *The Time Machine,* and a chronology of Wells's life. This is an excellent edition that can be warmly recommended to students.

Nicholas Ruddick's edition of *The Time Machine* was published by Broadview Press, Canada, in 2001. This incorporates the original Heinemann text of 1895 together with a range of useful supplementary material on the evolutionary context, the fourth dimension, and the fin de siècle. Ruddick's edition is valuable since it brings together in a convenient format a collection of material, including contemporary essays and reviews, that is not readily available elsewhere. Unfortunately, for copyright reasons this edition is not available in the United Kingdom.

Though based on rather different editorial principles, the editions edited by Parrinder and Ruddick point the way to future scholarship and bring together in an accessible format a reliably edited text and useful critical material.

H. G. WELLS'S PERENNIAL TIME MACHINE

The year 1995 marked the centenary of the original publication of *The Time Machine*. To mark the anniversary the H. G. Wells Society organized an International Symposium held at Imperial College, London, on the theme "*The Time Machine*: Past, Present and Future." The conference brought together Wells scholars from throughout the world. The proceedings were published in 2001 under the title *H. G. Wells's Perennial Time Machine*. This volume includes a range of papers assembled under the headings "Eternal Readability: A Work for All Time," "Currents of Its Time: Neoteny, Anthropology, Society, Numerology, Imperiality," and "The Rewriting: *The Time Machine* in the Twentieth Century and Beyond." Edited by George Slusser, Patrick Parrinder, and Danièle Chatelain, the handsomely produced centenary volume is a worthy tribute to the novel one hundred years after its initial publication. It says much for the vitality of *The Time Machine* that a century after its inception ninety scholars from many different nations could meet to discuss it both as a literary work, a prophetic narrative, and a contribution to modern ideas of time and evolution. In their introduction the editors note:

> Essentially, however, two groups will continue to debate it with renewed passion. Wellsian scholars, perennially intrigued by the relation of this first novel to the author's subsequent controversial works; and scientists, philosophers, and SF readers pursuing the elusive ways of time travel and the mystery of human time. Wells's work is, more than a "novel" or a "text," a great "invention." The Time Machine *was* necessary then. It has engaged the

> minds and imaginations of that virtual audience Wells was seeking in his new century. As we stand at the start of not just another century but a millennium, that audience will grow vaster in ways we cannot yet imagine.[25]

The editors are surely right to highlight the continuing significance of *The Time Machine* both as a literary work and as a seminal contribution to the history of ideas. As a literary text Wells's romance is now acknowledged as a founding cornerstone of modern science fiction, an essential reference point for all subsequent tales of time travel. As a contribution to the history of ideas it continues to fascinate and inspire, raising fundamental questions about evolution, progress, and human destiny. In a wider sense it raises speculations concerning the nature of the universe, the ultimate fate of our planet, and the nature of time itself. There is no reason to suppose that there will not be a continuing readership for the novel for as far into the future as we can foresee.

THE TIME MACHINE AND THE TWENTY-FIRST CENTURY

As we enter a new millennium, *The Time Machine* continues on its journey. At the time of writing we still await a definitive edition of Wells's text based on a close study of the holograph manuscript. Beyond this, there is scope for a wealth of critical approaches to the novel—including, for example, readings from feminist, Marxist, and structuralist standpoints.

Roland Barthes draws a useful distinction between two basic types of literary text: the readerly (lisible) and the writerly (scriptible). The readerly work is one that seems to offer a realistic picture of characters and scenes, a picture that does not require interpretation or analysis, since the meaning is conveyed in the text itself. The writerly text, in contrast, is one in which the meaning is less clear, a text that draws attention to its own fictionality and relies both on a surface narrative and a secondary narrative of imagery and metaphor. My thesis is that *The Time Machine* is a classic example of a writerly text, a text that will repay careful study because of its extensive use of symbolism, its mythological undertones, and the oblique relationship between author, narrator, reader, and text.

As we enter the new century the novel continues to exercise endless fascination on generations of readers. When Wells launched *The Time Machine* on its journey he can have had little inkling that the novel would itself become a kind of time machine, carrying his name into futurity.

NOTES

1. J. D. Beresford, *H. G. Wells* (London: Nisbet, 1915), 22–23.
2. Wells, *The War of the Worlds* (Heinemann, 1898), book 1, chap. 7.
3. Van Wyck Brooks, *The World of H. G. Wells* (London: Unwin, 1915), 34.
4. W. B. Pitkin, "Time and Pure Activity," *Journal of Philosophy, Psychology and Scientific Methods* 11 (1914): 521–26.
5. An example is the following sentence in chapter 11: "Far away up the desolate slope I heard a harsh scream, and saw a thing like a huge white butterfly go slanting and fluttering up into the sky and, circling, disappear into some low hillocks beyond." This sentence is identical in the Atlantic Edition, except that "into some low hillocks" has been replaced by "over some low hillocks."
6. Robert M. Philmus, ed., *The Island of Doctor Moreau: A Variorum Text* (Athens: University of Georgia Press, 1993).
7. "New Light on Mental Life" (1927), reprinted as chapter 19 in *The Way the World is Going* (Benn, 1928); "The Queer Story of Brownlow's Newspaper," *Strand* Magazine, 1932, reprinted in *The Complete Short Stories of H. G. Wells*, ed. John Hammond (London: Dent, 1998).
8. Anthony West, "H. G. Wells," in *Principles and Persuasions* (London: Eyre and Spottiswoode, 1958), 4–20, reprinted in Bernard Bergonzi, ed., *H. G. Wells: A Collection of Critical Essays* (Upper Saddle River, N.J.: Prentice Hall, 1976), 8–24.
9. The full text of Priestley's funeral address is included in Brian Ash, *Who's Who in H. G. Wells* (London: Elm Tree Books, 1979), 295–97.
10. Norman Nicholson, *H. G. Wells* (London: Arthur Barker, 1950), 27–28.
11. Bernard Bergonzi, *The Early H. G. Wells* (Manchester: Manchester University Press, 1961), 53, 61.
12. Cf., for example, the following passage from Samuel C. Chew and Richard D. Altick, *The Nineteenth Century and After* (London: Routledge and Kegan Paul, 1967), 156: "Wells's novels offer little interest to students of craftsmanship, for far from introducing innovations in the art of fiction, they generally exhibit a reversion to Victorian formlessness."
13. Robert M. Philmus, "The Logic of 'Prophecy,' in *The Time Machine*," *PMLA* 84 (1969), 530–35, reprinted in Bergonzi, ed., *H. G. Wells*, 56–68.
14. Darko Suvin, "A Grammar of Form and a Criticism of Fact," *Wellsian*, New Series [hereafter n.s.], no. 1 (1976): 18–33.
15. Norman and Jeanne Mackenzie, *The Time Traveller: The Life of H. G. Wells* (London: Weidenfeld and Nicolson, 1973), 122.
16. Wells, *Experiment in Autobiography* (London: Gollancz, 1934), 374.
17. Robert M. Philmus and David Y. Hughes, eds., *H. G. Wells: Early Writings in Science and Science Fiction* (Berkeley: University of California Press, 1975), 3.
18. Patrick Parrinder, "*The Time Machine*: H. G. Wells's Journey through Death," *Wellsian*, n.s., no. 4 (1981): 15–23.
19. John Huntington, *The Logic of Fantasy: H. G. Wells and Science Fiction* (New York: Columbia University Press, 1982), 41.

20. John Batchelor, *H. G. Wells* (Cambridge: Cambridge University Press, 1985), 14.

21. Bernard Loing, *H. G. Wells at Work* (Paris: Didier Erudition, 1984).

22. See for example, Philmus, ed., *The Island of Doctor Moreau,* and David Y. Hughes and Harry M. Geduld, eds., *A Critical Edition of The War of The Worlds* (Bloomington: Indiana University Press, 1993).

23. Michael Draper, *H. G. Wells* (London: Macmillan, 1987), 35, 42.

24. Harry M. Geduld, *The Definitive Time Machine* (Bloomington: Indiana University Press, 1987), 1.

25. George Slusser, Patrick Parrinder, and Danièle Chatelain, eds., *H. G. Wells's Perennial Time Machine* (Athens: University of Georgia Press, 2001), xv–xvi.

Index

About the Author

JOHN R. HAMMOND is a Research Fellow at Nottingham Trent University. His previous books include *H. G. Wells and the Modern Novel* (1988) and *H. G. Wells and the Short Story* (1992). He has also edited *The Complete Short Stories of H. G. Wells* (1998).